The Work
of the
Bond House

The Work
of the
Bond House

BY

LAWRENCE CHAMBERLAIN

BeardBooks

Washington, D.C.

Copyright 1912 by A. W. Ferrin

Reprinted 2000 by Beard Books, Washington, D.C.

ISBN 1-893122-76-X

Printed in the United States of America

PREFACE

ABOUT eighteen months ago Mr. Ferrin, the proprietor of MOODY'S MAGAZINE, requested me to write an article for his publication summarizing the services to the community that are performed by the American bond houses. It was his intention that men associated with other representative houses should write monographs on each separate bond house function. Their articles were to be elaborations of the several kinds of service that I had described in brief.

Whether because of engagements or reticence, the specialists in the various departments of the business, after reading my contribution in proof, suggested that the interest of a comprehensive and uniform presentation would best be served if I undertook the entire series, which I did. This is the explanation of the unusual form this book has taken.

While writing the articles I had no thought of making a book from them; but again I have been governed by suggestions from the bond houses. Certain of them wished the text in convenient form for distribution in quantity among their clients. If the articles bound are of some value for this purpose they may be of interest to the public in general; therefore this book.

These circumstances explain why a number of phrases, and perhaps even sentences and paragraphs, have been repeated in the following chapters, or have been taken from my book, *The Principles of Bond Investment,* that was published last year. Indeed the introductory chapter of this series was printed in that work.

I trust that I have faithfully presented bond house conditions as they are. If I have erred on the side of idealism, perhaps these pages will lead the public to require and a greater number of the investment houses to offer the quality of service I have described.

LAWRENCE CHAMBERLAIN.

Montclair, N. J., September 1, 1912.

CONTENTS

CHAPTER   PAGE

I. THE FUNCTIONS OF THE BOND HOUSES...... 9

    The Importance of the Bond Business—Ignorance of the Bond Business—Prevalence of Bond Buying in New England—Bankers vs. Brokers—The Functions of the Bond Houses—The Purchasing Function—The Advisory Function—The Banking Function—The Bond Houses as Fiscal Agents—The Selling Function—The Protective Function.

II. THE PURCHASING FUNCTION................ 28

    Bond Investment as a Science—Laboratory Methods—Special Counsel—One Man Buying—Financial Report Agencies—Railroads as Scientific Financiers—Buying to Satisfy Clients—The Professional Standard—The Effect of Interest Rates on Bond Buying—Stock Bonuses.

III. BUYING MUNICIPALS...................... 41

    The Ten Investment Elements—The Principal Function of the Bond Houses—Municipal Buying—The Buying of "Legals"—The Bond Attorney—The Selling Cost and Price of Legals—Carrying Charges—Unintelligent Proposals for Municipals—Municipal Bond Bureaus—General Market Municipals—Municipal Defaults.

CONTENTS

CHAPTER	PAGE

IV. BUYING RAILROAD BONDS.................. 56

> Common Characteristics of Railroad and Municipal Bonds—Railroad Bond Underwriting—Underwriting by Retail Houses—The Profits of Underwriting—A Pennsylvania Railroad Flotation — Railroad Blanket Refunding Issues — Equipment Bonds—Railroad Bond Investment—Proprietorship and Management—Community of Interest—Management—Physical Characteristics—Earning Power and Capitalization.

V. BUYING CORPORATION BONDS............... 74

> What Corporation Bonds Are—Classification of Bonds—Corporation Bond Investment Principles—Knowing the Business of the Corporation—Water Companies—Gas Companies—Street Railways—The Income of Public Service Corporations — Bond Houses as Specialists—The Newness of Corporation Bonds — Industrial Issues — The Competition for Public Utility Bonds—The Preference for Public Utilities—The Profit in Corporation Bonds—Costly Distribution—Construction Propositions—The Bond Houses as Reorganizers.

VI. THE ADVISORY FUNCTION.................. 91

> Advising a Woman—The Ethics of Salesmanship—Financial Jackals—English Selling Methods—Financial Advisory Systems

CONTENTS

—Bond Advertising—General Publicity—Advertising Investment Principles—Special Circulars—Investment by Correspondence.

VII. THE PROTECTIVE AND BANKING FUNCTIONS.. 104

The Mercantile vs. the Protective Policy—The Spirit of Trusteeship—Bond Guaranty—The Cost of the Guaranty—The Protective Function Applied to Marketability—The Cost to Clients of Artificial Marketability—Bonds as Collateral—The Banking Functions of the Bond Houses—The Cost to Bond Houses of Artificial Marketability—The Bond Houses as Banks of Deposit—The Protective Function Applied to all Bond Qualities—Protecting Security—Assuming Losses—Protection in Reorganization.

VIII. SELLING BONDS—THE BANKER'S VIEWPOINT. 119

The Development of Bond Selling—The Trouble with Bond Selling—The Cost of Selling—The Profit in Specialty Selling—Failures from Competition and Miscarriage of Issues—Selling Economies: Consolidation of Houses—Local Representation—Bank Representation—The Economy of Selling Collateral Trusts—Consolidation of Issues not Houses—The Selling Department of an Ideal Bond House—The Sales Manager—Territorial Managers—The Road Men — College Men as Salesmen — The Training of Green Men.

CONTENTS

CHAPTER	PAGE
IX. SELLING BONDS—THE INVESTOR'S VIEWPOINT	137

The Strength of the Investment Demand—Savings Banks as Bond Buyers—The Volume of Municipal Bond Sales—Annual Listings on the Exchange—The Obscure Issues—The Investor Should Know His Own Requirements—Complex Nature of Security — Complex Nature of Marketability—Second Consideration: Form of the Investment — Third Consideration: Proper Type of Bond—Fourth Consideration: The Proper Bond—Choosing a Bond House.

INDEX 150

CHAPTER I.

THE FUNCTIONS OF THE BOND HOUSES.

1. The Importance of the Bond Business. That part of the public which does not buy bonds has a very meagre idea of the importance and value to the community of the bond business. It is not necessary to resort to many figures. It is necessary only to realize that bonds are the chief resource of our government in times of war, of our states and municipalities in furtherance of public works and buildings, of our railroads, of almost all public service corporations and many industrial corporations. In round numbers $1,500,000,000 of American bonds are marketed every year and almost all of them pass through the hands of American bond houses. Even those issues of which the ultimate nominal market is the New York Stock Exchange are first offered and sponsored by dealers in bonds. In volume and number the transactions on the exchange are only a mere fraction of those in direct merchandising. Of this $1,500,000,000 of bonds one-third is absorbed by insurance companies, savings banks, trust companies and other banks (in approximately equal amounts)

10 FUNCTIONS OF BOND HOUSES

and the remaining two-thirds by corporations (for reserve, etc.) and by private investors in this country and abroad.

2. **Ignorance of the Bond Business.** In view of the vast importance of the bond business in the economic life of the country, it is somewhat surprising that so little is known about bonds and the bond business. No one who has had experience in selling bonds will deny that the "average man" who has accumulated a surplus is far more conversant with stocks and the basic principles of stock speculation than with bonds and the principles of bond investment. The reason, however, is not far to seek. While human nature remains what it is, the element of chance, with its exhilarating risk, will be more attractive to men than the element of approximate certainty that is arrived at by painstaking, uninspired care. Since the stock market is more interesting and problematical than the bond market to the majority of readers, journalism, in the course of its duty to purvey to the majority, perennially fills its financial pages with time-honored summaries of yesterday's exchange doings, to-day's gossip and circumspect conjectures as to the morrow.

3. **Prevalence of Bond Buying in New England.** Although, relatively speaking, the number of people at all conversant with bonds

FUNCTIONS OF BOND HOUSES 11

is small through the country at large, it is sometimes surprising to find what a large proportion of the well-to-do in the Northeastern States, which have been educated to bond buying, have at some time or other bought bonds. Every Eastern bond house has, or ought to have, a list of at least 70 per cent of all the bond buyers of consequence in every city or town in New England. A comparison of this list with a list of all persons estimated to be worth $50,000 or more, whether bond buyers or not, will prove the prevalence of bond buying in this section.

4. Bankers vs. Brokers. The leading banking houses were not always primarily bond houses. Two generations ago financial business of all kinds was transacted by "bankers and brokers." Bond selling was an incident to the general banking, exchange and brokerage routine. It was all done "over the counter." There was comparatively little implied responsibility on the part of the vendor. In the age of Commodore Vanderbilt, the elder Gould, Fisk and Drew the "caveat emptor" principle of exchange was accepted and the devil took many beside the hindmost. But now the speculative business in New York, so far as it is reputable and consequential, is done by "Members of the New York Stock Exchange" and the investment business is done by "Bankers, Dealers in Investment Bonds." Of course, a house marketing investment securities may have a seat on one of the exchanges, but it is accepted and understood that the firm specializes in one or the other of these two forms of business. The financial atmosphere, the financial temper and the training necessary to superior service in either occupation have accomplished the severance of stock dealing and bond selling.

5. **The Functions of the Bond Houses.** Of course the primary function of the bond house is to obtain capital for the creation of new enterprises or the enlargement of old. So far as concerns these houses in their proper capacity the capital obtained is in the form of loans. The houses purchase the loans outright for their own account and resell to their clients. As in any sort of merchandising, there are few wholesalers and many retailers. The prominent "wholesale" bond dealers, numbering less than a dozen, hitherto have confined themselves for the most part (as far as American corporation loans are concerned) to the great railroad systems. There are signs that the policy will be broadened in the near future. These houses have few, if any, traveling representatives. Their sales, in this country, are effected by public subscription, stimulated through extensive advertising, and by distribution to large

FUNCTIONS OF BOND HOUSES 13

investment institutions, such as the insurance companies, and to the smaller bond houses.

6. We are not justified in omitting to state that the wholesale international bankers have not been trained by the necessities of the personal relation between client and financial advisor to accept and offer only such securities as they would be willing to keep for their own account. It is not necessary to illustrate, but none of the typical American "retail" bond houses could have the hold many of them do have upon their customers if they had recommended and sold a tithe of the bonds *and stocks* that have been distributed by some of the international bankers. Mere magnitude in the capitalization of a bond house or of an obligor corporation is still a thing to conjure with in America. Financial history does not support the view that there is safety in size, except with respect to municipal corporations. Since the international houses, with special spheres of usefulness, do not best represent the things for which the bond houses stand, and since the contact of private investors is with representatives of the retail houses, this work is concerned only with the latter.

7. "Retail" is not a term properly descriptive of the firms we have in mind, although it suggests the relative size of the issues handled and the relative volume of business. It mis-

leads if it suggests that the main business of such houses is to distribute among small investors issues that originally were investigated and purchased by "wholesale" houses. This is not the case. For the most part each of the American bond houses buys its issues independently, in accordance with its policy regarding investments, or it buys them "in joint account" with other houses having similar policies. These houses are autonomous; their prosperity is built on their ability to find and obtain, on the one hand, funded obligations that merit investment, and on the other, a clientele that has faith in them and their business judgment and probity.

8. The success of the bond houses in weathering all sorts of financial storms while stock exchange houses have gone down by the score, is strong support of the contention that bond investment rests on a basis of principles reducible to a science. The writer knows of not one important investment house that has failed except through deliberate violation of perfectly well-known investment principles or through equally deliberate fraud. There is no business in all the country that has placed itself on more enduring foundations of business wisdom, or that is conducted on a higher plane of business ethics.

9. Enough has been said to imply the great

FUNCTIONS OF BOND HOUSES 15

services of the American bond houses. Without their help it would be impossible to finance American enterprises upon equally favorable terms. By their ultra-conservatism they are establishing themselves in public confidence in a way to bring together with the greatest expedition and least middleman's cost the promoters of our national resources and the creditor classes from which must come the capital necessary to municipal and industrial development. They extend the boundaries of credit and exercise a directive and steadying influence upon enterprise. By preaching the principles of bond buying in advertisements, pamphlets, correspondence, and in personal interviews by bond salesmen they are slowly but surely converting the American people into a nation of investors. When the rest of the country can acquire, to a degree, the thrift of New Englanders we shall be referred to the Dutch and French less frequently, and our industrial structure will be no longer in unstable equilibrium. It will be worth while to examine in greater detail the several functions these houses perform.

10. **The Purchasing Function.** If a municipal loan is to be offered, the purchase is a comparatively simple matter, provided the municipality is well known to the fraternity. Then no preliminary investigation is required;

16 FUNCTIONS OF BOND HOUSES

a bid is made for the loan at the current market rates and acceptance on award is subject to the approval of the bidder's attorney in all respects affecting the validity of the obligation.

11. If the municipality is not well known to the bidder a qualified representative will be, or should be, sent to learn at first hand the physical and financial condition of the city and to form an estimate of its probable future willingness and ability to meet its present and future obligations.

12. If a corporation loan is offered probably it will be submitted at the offices of the bankers by a representative of the company or by a promoter. If the applicant is of a social turn of mind he is not likely to lack the company of his kind in the ante-room. Competition, fortunately, is fairly active.

13. The first step in the process of elimination (there is more elimination than acceptance) is to discard the propositions of companies that conduct a kind of business unfamiliar to the bankers. Except under unusually favorable circumstances the highest grade of bond houses will not purchase bonds of industrial corporations, mining or irrigation companies, etc.

14. The next step is to discard loans that have not a claim on property worth, under the most unfavorable conditions, more than the

FUNCTIONS OF BOND HOUSES 17

amount of the obligation secured. Most corporations will bond themselves in as large a sum as their bankers will permit. Loans are continually being rejected because of insufficient equity in property values.

15. The third step is to discard those propositions which do not give reasonable assurance of earning at all times at least 50 per cent more than all fixed charges, after making extremely liberal estimates for depreciation and future increased operating expenses.

16. The fourth step is to decline loans to companies conducted by men or with methods that do not meet with approval.

If the banking house is satisfied by interview and correspondence in matters of the above nature, and if a suitable price can be agreed upon, then engineers and accountants may be sent to the plant and offices to make a thorough examination; and the members of the firm, with counsel, meet officers of the company and their attorneys to settle the matters of form. On acceptance of an issue a careful banking house may demand representation on the directorate of the company until such time as the company shall have discharged its bonded obligation.

17. Illustrative of the care with which properties are examined, the writer recently had occasion to inspect an interurban line in Penn-

sylvania and incident to mileage cost of construction inquired in jest the number of ties between the terminal and a certain city some miles distant. "We don't know," replied one of the owners of the road, "ask your engineer, Mr. ————. He has photographs of every foot of the line and can count the ties for you, but probably he has already counted them."

18. Of course there is a difference in the degree of care exercised by various houses. The ultra-conservative will not permit their names to be associated with "construction propositions." They will consider for purchase the obligations only of seasoned companies with established earning power.

19. The reactionary effect of the stringent requirements of bond houses is of inestimable benefit to corporation finance, but its good influence has a wider sphere: it embraces municipal corporations and municipal finance. American bond houses have put municipal bond buying on an entirely different plane from what it was in 1875. In this they have been helped by, and have helped, the development of municipal bond law. In these days cities and towns that have had much experience placing bonds will be certain in advance of their advertisements for bids that the loan has been issued in conformity with the exacting requirements of the bond attorneys. Certain

strong Canadian houses command such respect in their country that they have been able to direct the legislation of the Western provinces to the end that the Western loans may be more acceptable to the investors in the Eastern provinces and in England.

20. **The Advisory Function.** This advisory and directive function, however, is more prominently operative in bond selling than in bond buying. It has its source in the statistical departments which every house of quality must maintain. It finds its chief expression, as already stated, in tabloid investment lessons, printed in the advertising columns of newspapers and periodicals, or with somewhat greater fullness in pamphlets and monographs. If a prospective client has an investment policy that apparently is not suited to his particular needs, the home office may tactfully direct his attention by letter or through their representative in his territory to a means by which he may better his position. Some bond houses maintain a daily news sheet for the benefit of their salesmen in which are printed not only pertinent items of current interest, but timely discussions of different problems.

21. Activities of this nature, developed to their logical conclusion, can lead to only one result, the establishment of the American bond houses in the confidence of the public as their

chief advisers in financial matters, in some such relation as the great banks of France and Germany bear to investors in those countries. Even now a few of the better houses can count upon the absorption by their friends among institutions and investors of a certain amount of any issue they recommend and offer.

22. This advisory function can become general and economically sound only as the bond houses as a class recognize the *scientific* and *professional* nature of their calling and guide their movements and policies, as do the governors of the Bank of England, let us say, alive to the power of their position and their responsibility as repositories of a nation's confidence.

23. **The Banking Function.** Illustrative of the confidential relation between house and client, there has arisen the demand that banking departments be established for the safe keeping of funds destined, upon enlargement, to go into investment, and also to accommodate those who wish to purchase securities before they have sufficient funds to pay in full for them. From the necessities of these two situations it is only a short step to the conduct on a small scale of a bank of deposit subject to check. But properly and ordinarily, the banking department of a bond house is conducted as a matter of accommodation to its customers, and

FUNCTIONS OF BOND HOUSES

not primarily to do a general banking business. From these beginnings it sometimes has happened that a full-fledged bank has been evolved, in which the savings, deposit and trust functions of the bank have balanced, nominally at least, the sales function of the bond house, but an exception of this sort would only prove the rule. Although bond houses are banks, technically, and are entitled to their common designation, "bankers," nevertheless, on the principle that security selling is not best undertaken by obligor companies but is properly left to the bond houses which make it a profession, so the general banking business is best left to banks proper.

24. The Bond Houses as Fiscal Agents. Because of their purchasing, advisory and banking functions the bond houses are called upon to act as fiscal agents for corporations, municipalities and even states. The long standing, friendly banking relations of the older firms with the Western cities recall the fact that interest, and sometimes the principal, of the loans of these cities is payable at the offices of the bond house. Here and there an Eastern institution is met that will not buy Western municipals which are not payable in the East. This is not so much to save the cost of conversion into New York funds, for that might be arranged in the price, as because of the

22 FUNCTIONS OF BOND HOUSES

inconvenience and possible loss of interest in shipping the bonds west for collection. Some of the older bond houses act as depositaries for Western cities. In general, the conduct of the bond houses as fiscal agents has merited the trust placed in them.

25. It is more to be expected that private corporations will look to the bond houses as their financial agents. The disposition of a company's funded loans is not merely a matter of merchandising; it is natural that the relationship begun by the purchase of bonds and banking representation on the directorate shall be continued indefinitely in the thought of future financial needs. Just as the great railroad systems have their long established financial connections with certain large houses, so the public service and other private corporations form alliances with the bond houses. The continuance of such relations implies conformity on the part of the obligor corporations with the policy of the bond houses. This also tends toward a betterment of financial conditions throughout the country.

26. **The Selling Function.** American banking houses are not eleemosynary. Whatever may be their usefulness in the community, it is the result of that enlightened self-interest which used to be expressed in the phrase "Honesty is the best policy." Their reason

FUNCTIONS OF BOND HOUSES 23

for being is to make money by selling bonds, and the competition is getting keener every day. Many of the ordinary effects of competition are noticeable in the bond business. There is standardization of wares and policies, there is diminution in ratio of profits. But two ordinary effects of competition are conspicuously absent. There is no deterioration of the product and no tendency toward consolidation among the vendors.

27. The relation of supply and demand for securities is totally different with us from what it is in England or France. Our industrial development more than keeps pace with our investment resources. We are less dependent on foreign capital than ever before, but not so rich that funds awaiting conservative employment have not a choice of excellent opportunities at home.

28. By reason of this very competitive bidding by capital the quality of our loan product offered by good bond houses is not cheapened. In the process of soliciting business by advertisement and interview, American investors are becoming educated in investment principles and reward with most patronage the houses that give the best evidence of living up to investment ideals. It is the same in this as in the legal and medical professions. It pays best in the long run to be technically competent.

29. Since the principal point of contact between investors and banking houses is through travelling representatives whose advice is followed to a very material extent by the investors, the salesmen sent out are of more than average intelligence and business ability. The large majority of those representing the better concerns are college bred men. The alert sales manager will keep in touch with the colleges and universities and will seek to obtain for his firm men of the graduate schools or of the graduating class who give promise of ability in salesmanship not only by their record in college activities but by their appearance and address. Most of these men will serve office apprenticeships of length before they are sent out on the road.

30. The other usual effect of competition that we mentioned as lacking is the tendency toward consolidation. The absence of it is further evidence of the peculiarly professional relation which subsists between the banking house in its advisory capacity and the client. It raises bond selling from a business to a profession.

31. There are some who profess to see in the gradual evolution of the bond business a tendency to relinquish direct selling from house to client through travelling salesmen in favor of distribution, on a commission basis,

FUNCTIONS OF BOND HOUSES 25

through local independent bankers. This may come. If it should, it would be one of the evil effects of competition. It would relieve the "retail" houses of a large part of that sense of personal responsibility which they now feel. They would be in a position analogous to that of the wholesale houses at present. Investors would have to accept offerings from those who had no part in the investigation which preceded the original purchase of the issue, and who, presumably, would not have the capital or organization of distribution to "protect the market" for the benefit of those who might wish subsequently to sell their securities.

32. **The Protective Function.** There is a radical difference in the attitude of different bond houses in this matter of repurchasing securities of clients to whom they have sold them. Some take the stand that a sale is a sale, and the responsibility of a house that has acted in good faith ceases upon delivery of the bond and the receipt of payment. This position is logical and just, but again competition steps in to benefit the customer. Other houses say: "We shall put out our issues as nearly as possible on a plane of marketability with active listed securities. We make no promises, but, except in times of panic when it may be impossible to raise money to satisfy

26 FUNCTIONS OF BOND HOUSES

everybody, we hope and expect to be so situated as to buy back at the fair market price the securities we have sold." The substance of this statement is now occasionally seen in advertisements over the signature of some of the better and stronger houses. Few investors realize the full significance of this protective market policy. They are inclined to remember that they may buy most of the active listed bonds on the exchange and sell them the same day at an average total loss, due to the "higgling of the market," of perhaps only 2 points or so. They do not realize that on a declining bond market they may have to take an additional loss, in listed bonds, of say 8 points, or 10 points in all, whereas in the same circumstance a bond house would think twice before quoting a client a price 10 points below the previous selling price. And, to say nothing of investment guidance, nine times out of ten the issue of the bond house is yielding at least ½% more per annum than an equally sound listed issue.

33. But the protective function of the bond house is most important in respect to the moral responsibility of "seeing clients through" default, reorganization and rehabilitation in the extremely rare cases in which trouble arises. In some instances losses amounting to hundreds of thousands of dollars have been

FUNCTIONS OF BOND HOUSES 27

made good; in many instances the firms have volunteered to pay interest which has been suspended; in every case a reputable bond house will feel called upon to take active leadership in upholding the mortgage rights or other legal claims of the bondholders.

34. The creditor class will do well to take as much pains in the investment of its wealth as in the acquisition of it. Buyers of corporation bonds should exercise almost as much care in the selection of a financial adviser as in the choice of a security. They should seek a bond house with a strong personality, strong convictions on investment matters and the capital and equipment to back them up.

The chapters following will discuss, in detail, the several functions that have been touched only briefly here in order to present, at first, the bird's-eye view.

CHAPTER II.

THE PURCHASING FUNCTION.

35. Bond Investment as a Science. It is only as one studies the purchasing function of the bond houses, and the achievements and possibilities of economic service through the process of selection in purchases, that one realizes how rapidly bond investment is growing into a well-defined and thoroughly developed science. Then why not treat the principles of bond investment in scholarly fashion and credit the orderly study of them as the Science of Bond Investment? We hear much these days of scientific management in manufacture and transportation. It is a wonderful and profitable thing; witness the Standard Oil Company and the Atchison, Topeka and Santa Fé. The greater pity that below Fulton Street a man who speaks of science and finance in the same breath carries the reproach of being theoretical.

36. However, the attitude of Wall Street is changing toward those whose profession it is to know securities. One of the greatest houses on the street may still have no statistical department, except that which is carried home nights under one or two well-rounded

THE PURCHASING FUNCTION

hats; but, on the other hand, a firm of national reputation and esteem has recently admitted into partnership a man whose claim to the distinction is his profound railroad scholarship. The traditions and methods of the dry goods and clothing merchants who founded our financial institutions in New York, are giving way as the younger college-bred generation, trained in, or at least in sympathy with scientific methods, advances to influential administrative positions.

37. **Laboratory Methods.** Scientific method in bond buying presupposes well-equipped laboratories and trained analysts. I have the good fortune to be familiar with the organization and work of one of the best financial laboratories in New York. The nucleus from which it has developed is the statistical department. This is in charge of a man who fattens on income accounts and balance sheets. He is prepared, if necessary, with a defensible ex cathedra report and opinion on almost any company or security that has a vogue in the Street. He directs a group of assistants in the compilation and analysis of ten-year records of all American corporations of note. So far as these records relate to public service and industrial companies, they are not and cannot be built up from any standard framework, but each is shaped out of the characteristics of the

particular business and the nature of the meagre material that usually offers.

38. In behalf of the statistician and his collaborators, the library shelves are weighted with bound volumes of company mortgages, corporation reports, gazettes, financial periodicals and technical journals. The atlases, annuals, institutional directories, current quotation sheets and dividend notices of two continents are at his elbow. He has standing orders with the second-hand book dealers for works that are out of print—old railroad surveys, special monographs—and all new publications that have even a collateral bearing on his work, are submitted as soon as published.

39. **Special Counsel.** The firm that avails itself of this systematic service also retains special counsel, who give their entire time to the legal problems that are constantly incident to the prosecution of business affairs of scale. Likewise an engineer is retained for consultation regarding the physical aspects of properties with which the firm has, or contemplates, affiliation. The list of consultants and department specialists by no means ends with these advisers. Others, with experience in syndicate association, accounting, and management, or with developed sense of market values, or of intrinsic investment values, are at hand for the immediate help that their particular training and aptitude makes possible.

THE PURCHASING FUNCTION 31

40. One Man Buying. I happen to know fairly well, also, the buying department of a bond house that has not yet grown to the size admitting this admirable specialization. In this smaller house all enterprises requiring new capital must be investigated by one man with the slight statistical help obtainable from a clerk or two. Any proposition that secures his conditional approval is submitted in due course to outside engineers and lawyers, and ultimately lacks nothing in the nature of protection to investors that special facilities and professional training can contribute. Not because of the lawyers and engineers, primarily, but because of the character of the investigator himself, I would trust to the safety of the bonds this firm offers as implicitly as to that of similar bonds of any other house in the Street.

This merely illustrates what we all know, that elaborate specialization and scientific methods are supplements of, not substitutes for old-fashioned horse sense and business judgment.

41. That this smaller house has no well-articulated statistical department is not because of narrow unbelief—far from it—but because it must perform all its functions according to scale: its buying must bear definite relation to its selling. The handicaps of such houses as this are infinitely less, however, than they were a half-dozen years ago. Their disadvantage has been lessened by the growth of the scientific spirit itself, in the Street. It is no mean labor, for instance, to assemble and catalog the several hundred more prominent railroad mortgages. If one offers for sale railroad bonds without having digested the mortgage securing them, one is grossly negligent. Yet it is very difficult to obtain copies of many mortgages after they have been in existence a few years.

42. **Financial Report Agencies.** There are now several financial agencies—bad, indifferent and good—that correspond in some respects to the commercial agencies in the world of trade, and supply the materials on which may be based intelligent judgments of corporations and their securities. Among them are railroad bond description agencies that furnish correct texts of railroad mortgages, or at least the essential recitals, and maps that show the exact incidence of each mortgage on the road's track and the relation of each mortgage to every other, as to priority of lien.

43. **Statistical Material.** Very few people in the bond business, even bond statisticians themselves, realize the amount and quality of statistical help that is at the service of all, but that is particularly serviceable to small

THE PURCHASING FUNCTION 33

houses which are unprepared to do research work over the entire bond field. Some of the best aid is from the Government and may be had for the asking. The most comprehensive works on American telephony and street railroading are the latest Special Census Reports on these subjects, published three or four years ago.

44. The matter of special statistical service need not be entered into further here. It will be taken up again in discussing the buying of various types of bonds. There is, however, a general financial service of vast importance not only to bond buyers but to all classes of business men. This is the service that aims to depict accurately and clearly the financial health of this country and of the world at large; but more important still, to indicate positively whether the underlying conditions that govern the movement of prices are tending toward betterment or not. The quality of work done by those committed to this type of service varies extremely. Some of it is unreliable; some of it gives evidence of a high degree of statistical scholarship.

45. It will be admitted that if scientific methods and the scientific spirit can apply themselves to business affairs with such effect as to produce dependable prophets of the financial future, the mouth of criticism will be

stopped. About a year ago I was discussing with the vice-president of one of the Wall Street national banks the very intimate relation between the course of active listed bond prices and the ratio of loans to deposits in the national banks of the country—both expressions of credit conditions—and suggested to him the possibility of building an antecedent chart from banking and other credit conditions that would determine this ratio of loans to deposits and therefore determine at any time the advisability of entering the market to buy bonds. The subject was of such importance that I was encouraged with an offer of assistance, and even collaboration, which I could not accept at the time. Fortunately this labor has now been saved and the object apparently attained by others more competent and better equipped than I for such work.

46. Let it be said for the benefit of business men in general that studies into fundamental conditions can be related to any business. Certain sets of statistics will have more weight in some activities than in others. Presumably immigration figures are of more immediate interest to steamship companies than to railroads, and crop conditions of more interest to railroads than to steamship companies; but country-wide prosperity is of immediate interest to all, and so also is the price-level.

In so far as success in any business is separated from failure by the purchase of materials, labor and capital when they are cheap and the sale of them when they are dear, success is to be won by deference to a reliable and comprehensive system of financial service. Bond buyers are only one among many classes that may be benefited.

47. Railroads as Scientific Financiers. It is natural that the railroads should first awake to the possibility of really scientific financing. Their association with bankers and banking principles is so intimate and of such long standing that they have become conversant with the art of buying and selling capital. They buy long-time credit far in excess of immediate needs when money is plenty, and short-time credit at higher rates when money is scarce. The New Haven Road is especially alert to take advantage of changing interest conditions. Of late the example of the railroads has been followed by other large corporations. In either case the less sophisticated investing public are willing to seize the short end of the exchange. With the growth in power to diagnose fundamental conditions all business men at least will be on the same plane of opportunity to profit by the revolutions of the trade cycle.

48. Buying to Satisfy Clients. The buyer of

bonds for a banking house has other big general problems besides these concerning the proper time and price for making commitments. The wares he offers for sale must be suited to the needs of his clientele. To a certain extent he may modify these needs. He may "educate the taste" of his patrons. To a certain extent he may seek the patronage of the class of investors who want the kind of thing he is willing to sell. If he is a big man, and his wares are not moving as rapidly as they should, he may change his entire selling program—he will do almost anything but take a deliberate risk for which his customers, and therefore his house, must ultimately pay.

49. **The Professional Standard.** Perhaps many, whether engaged in financial work or not, will consider the investment standard too idealistic—impossible of maintenance outside of print. This is absolutely wrong. My own bond associations have been largely with houses that refuse to take what appear to be speculative risks, and my experience is not exceptional. To be sure, there is nothing illegitimate in the assumption of risk or in the offer of speculative paper by firms engaged in that kind of business; but deliberate hazard or avoidable speculation are foreign to the better American retail bond houses.

50. There is a firm operating in the East, whose senior members have grown gray in

the selling of savings bank bonds. In the past this policy yielded adequate profits, an enviable reputation, and, not least, the satisfaction of never having sold a security that occasioned loss. But the profit in savings bank bonds, always relatively narrow, has lessened considerably in recent years by increased competition. The patronage of a savings bank can no more be monopolized than that of private investors, for the nature of "legal" securities makes almost superfluous the endorsement of the vendor. So competition in savings banks selling is of the freest kind, and a house that specializes in it has no insuperable advantage over a house that caters to more diversified and profitable patronage. A change of bond-buying policy is possible in this house and others similarly situated, upon the retirement of senior interests, but the problem is vital and requires ultimate solution.

51. There is, on the other hand, a house not confined to Eastern selling that some years ago changed its major financial associations because of a difference of opinion as to what constituted "legitimate" issues. For a while it was reasonably successful in disposing of a class of securities in which there was a very wide margin of profit, but for which there was no general market at all. This firm is now confronted with a dissatisfied and diminished clientele and the difficult task of rehabilitating

a threadbare reputation by return to old-line securities.

52. The Boston bond firms, as a whole, have to meet a new and serious difficulty arising from the increased activities of Massachusetts assessors. The tax rate in Massachusetts ranges close to 2 per cent. Undoubtedly there is a greater amount of security investment per capita in Massachusetts than in any other State in the Union. Consequently, tax-exempt bonds seldom yield $3\frac{1}{2}$ per cent., and yet a bond on which taxes are paid must yield $5\frac{1}{2}$ per cent.—in other words, must be at least second grade, to suffer the tax and make return equivalent to tax-exempt bonds.

53. It is well enough to deplore the short-sightedness of legislation that handicaps investment and encourages speculation, but the bond houses must meet conditions as well as theories. As the result of this Massachusetts situation the Boston bond houses are beginning to handle the stocks of Massachusetts corporations, which are tax-exempt within the State. In some cases these stocks are not mentioned in the general circulars of the bond houses, but are sold entirely by personal solicitation. In New York, as we all know, one or two bond houses of high repute publicly advertise for sale the preferred stocks of industrial companies. Will this practice become general, and if so, will it alter the confidential relation

THE PURCHASING FUNCTION 39

between firm and client that has been established at such pains?

54. The Effect of Interest Rates on Bond Buying. A cause more general than the activity of tax assessors has been at work for the past few years compelling a shift of sentiment and policy in bond buying, namely, the rise in interest rates. This is a phenomenon that MOODY'S MAGAZINE has the distinction of first bringing to public attention in this country. Elsewhere I take issue with the extreme stand of some of MOODY's contributors who see little in the advance of rates except the effect of an increased annual production of gold.* There is not space here to rehearse the controversy, but it is of importance to bond houses in shaping their buying policy and their methods of financing corporations to know whether this advance in rates is founded on permanent conditions that must be recognized and met, or on transitory circumstances such as an excessive tariff and congestion of population, that may disappear before it is necessary to adopt radical changes in selling policy to meet them.

55. If the good railroad refunding issues are permanently headed from a 4 per cent. to a 4½ per cent. basis it may mean that inactive public service bonds hitherto worth a 5½ per cent. basis, will be worth only a 6 per

---
*Note. The Principles of Bond Investment, chapter on "The Future of Bond Prices."

40 THE PURCHASING FUNCTION

cent. basis. This in turn may mean the vogue of 6 per cent. bonds selling at about par rather than 5 per cent. bonds selling at a discount; or it may mean a 5 per cent. bond with a stock bonus. Apart from the unholiness of stock in general, once the investor gets the bonus habit he is hard to cure. It is still a sign of transition in interest rates, not a sign of benevolence or necessity, when stock is "given away" with bonds. When trading stamps are of economic benefit to trade, stock bonuses will be to finance.

56. **Stock Bonuses.** Yet this in turn, is hardly a fair statement. Stock bonuses come to the bond house in part payment for the capital loaned, and the offer of these bonuses to clients is merely the offer to share prospective profits from future operations of the obligated company. It is sounder financing, however, for the bond house to charge less for the capital it loans, when it buys the bonds, and to offer the bonds to its clients at a correspondingly lower figure. I believe that, in the long run, more is lost than gained by encouraging speculative interest from the ultimate furnishers of investment capital.

57. Enough has been said to outline the gravity of general bond buying problems. The succeeding chapter will deal with the purchasing function in relation to particular types of public and private corporation loans.

CHAPTER III.

BUYING MUNICIPALS.

58. The previous chapters outlined some of the principal problems and kinds of assistance, statistical and advisory, that are met in the routine of bond buying. It is left to differentiate the problems and helps that apply to particular types of bonds.

59. **The Ten Investment Elements.** In the first place, we must come to some conclusions regarding the investment qualities we seek in examining the loans submitted for purchase. A careful survey of all possible excellences yields us ten elements for the ideal investment.[1]

Security of principal.
Stability of income (or security of interest).
A fair return.
Marketability. ⎫ Convertibility.
Value as collateral. ⎭
Tax exemption.
Freedom from care.
Acceptable duration.
Acceptable denomination.
Possibility of appreciation.

60. Whether the possibility of appreciation is not purely a speculative quality may be open

---

[1] The Elements of an Ideal Investment, Chapter III of The Principles of Bond Investment.

to discussion, but otherwise the list is probably unquestionable and comprehensive. We may say then that if a bond house can obtain for its clients an issue with (1) principal reasonably secure, (2) interest payments regular and certain, (3) a fair return in income, (4) a fairly responsive market, (5) hypothecary value at the banks—an issue, (6) that is free from direct tax, and (7) requires merely semi-annual coupon clipping, and (8) matures after a satisfactory lapse of time, and (9) comes in convenient units of denomination (small for the frugal poor, and large for the rich, so as not to crowd the strong box), and (10) has as good a chance of appreciating as of depreciating when its qualities become more generally recognized—well, a bond house cannot furnish such an issue, for it does not exist.*

61. Evidently, then, there is plenty of room for discrimination and selective judgment in bond buying. Incidentally, however, is there any other kind of investment that will so nearly meet these ten requirements? Will mortgages?

62. The three investment qualities that receive the most consideration are security, income, and marketability. Obviously all three cannot exist in a high degree in the same

---

*Note. The Principles of Bond Investment, Chapter on "The Elements of an Ideal Investment."

BUYING MUNICIPALS

paper. If the investment is safe it cannot return a high rate of interest and at the same time have a broad and active market, for such a market implies competitive demand, and the competition for a security that was at once of safe and high yield would immediately bid up the price and thus lower the yield.

63. Therefore, assuming a good security, the first problem of the bond house is the choice it must make for its specialization between large transactions with small profits in issues with broad markets, and small transactions with much larger profits in issues without vogue or reputation.

64. **The Principal Function of the Bond Houses.** If, because of prejudice, or want of knowledge concerning its qualities, an issue is without vogue, and has to be sold painstakingly by personal solicitation, it may be both safe and of high return. *It is the principal and thoroughly commendable function of the better American bond houses to sell to their clients issues of bonds which have unimpeachable security and yet an income considerably higher than would be the case were the issues well known to the investing public.*

65. Setting aside United States bonds, which (with the possible exception of the insular issues) are not truly investment paper, we have as representative of security, vogue and

market, at the expense of income, the great body of American Civil Loans, viz., state, county, city and town, and tax district bonds.

66. At the opposite extreme, representative of reasonable security and greater income, at the expense of vogue or market, we have public service corporation bonds, and some "industrials."

67. In the middle ground are railroad bonds, offering, as a class, less security than civil loans, more than public utility loans, and inclining toward marketability rather than income. Let us consider each of these classes in turn.

68. **Municipal Buying.** History makes rapidly in civil bond law. If it were not for the Riddlebergers, the Tennessee Settlements, and a few others, Wall Street would have forgotten before this that nine states repudiated their debts between 1870 and 1884. The constitutions and statutes of so many commonwealths now forbid the incurrence of more than nominal state debt, and the loans that do issue are of such special market, that these, as well as the governments, may be omitted from this brief discussion.

69. The problem of buying the other civil loans, the municipals proper and the quasi-municipals such as county and tax district bonds, may be divided according to the charac-

BUYING MUNICIPALS 45

ter of their investment destination. From the business point of view municipals are broadly either "legals" or "general market" bonds.

70. **The Buying of "Legals."** By "legals," of course, are meant municipals that conform to the high requirements of the older, richer states governing the investment of savings bank deposits and trust funds. In the nature of the case the legals are, in general, superior to the general market municipals.

71. In purchasing legals the question of security is almost nil. No banking house, for instance, would or could be held morally responsible for the default of any municipal issue that is a legal investment for the savings banks of Massachusetts or New York. Legality for savings bank investment and legality of issuance by the municipality are entirely distinct matters. The questions of legality of issuance and validity are quite apart from those of the financial competency or the good faith of a city. It is not a function of the bond houses to establish legality of issuance but that of their attorneys. It may astonish many to learn that a record of sales I kept in 1907, of the more important municipal issues of that year, shows that of a total of $200,000,000 of municipal and state bonds issued, some $4,000,000 or 2 per cent., divided among 65 loans, were finally declined by those who had pur-

chased them subject to approval of counsel; and usually, but not always, declined on the ground that the issue was invalid because of some lack of compliance with minor requirements of law. This $4,000,000 does not take into account a very much larger amount of issues that the attorney of the purchaser found insufficiently protected by law, but that by further acts at his suggestion, the issuing community was able to validate completely without formal resale.

72. The Bond Attorney. Not all bond attorneys, however, are competent. Even an apparently "legal" municipal may be unsafe if its validity has been passed upon by a lawyer who is more interested in making immediate profits for his client the bond house, than considerate for his reputation and its future welfare. Any bond house dealing in municipals can name certain attorneys whose "legal opinion" is worthless in its eyes because of incompetence or lack of scruple. Not long ago one such attorney in New York State accepted as valid an issue of bonds signed by a man who had never been appointed or elected to the office designated under his signature.

It is the business of the bond house to protect its clients against the work of these charlatans. They are very few and far between, and lower but little the high plane of legal skill and ethics that are devoted to safeguarding American bond issues.

73. **The Selling Cost and Price of Legals.** The buying of legals as a mercantile rather than legal problem narrows down to technical skill in sensing the current demand and steering the bid in that very narrow channel of profit that lies between the Scylla of competitive bids and the Charybdis of too high an asking price.

It is easier to guess what price the bonds will bring when sold to the public, than what price the other houses will bid at the public sale; but conceding the municipal buyer could be fairly certain of both, he is not yet saved. He must compute the selling cost to him per bond, and be sure, humanly speaking, of a margin of profit. How many houses do this? How many of the two thousand bond firms in the United States have any intelligent cost accounting? It may be interesting to know that a certain house that does a large and very general bond business throughout the country computes the selling cost at nearly $14 a $1,000 bond. This includes the cost of the slow moving "specialties," but also the cost of mere brokerage transactions on which the profit may be only 1-32, or 31 cents a bond.

74. At the present time the *gross* profit in selling legal municipals surely does not exceed

$10 a bond or one per cent. I believe it is not over $7.50 a bond. If these statements of costs and profits are approximately correct, are the bond houses charging too much for the services they perform? If these statements are correct, are institutions and individuals ordinarily wise in bidding direct for bonds at public sale, rather than accepting the established market after the sale? The answer will be found by study of the list of bidders, and the amounts bid, in any sale of New York City bonds. If these statements are correct, are municipalities wise in trying to sell their loans, bond by bond, "over the counter," rather than by paying, as a matter of economy, the middleman's profit?

75. Carrying Charges. It would not be possible for houses to live on such small profits if the bonds did not in the long run "carry themselves," i. e., produce a sufficient coupon income to offset the interest charges of their hypothecation at the banks. A diamond or wool merchant, it is to be observed, or a merchant in any other commodity, has not this advantage of a self-supporting collateral.

76. With a gross one per cent. profit, that may be wiped out by a change in the market conditions, it is essential that the bidding for legal municipals should be most circumspect. With this in view a properly equipped house

BUYING MUNICIPALS

will keep on its books a record of past bidding for all municipal issues of consequence. This record will show the amount of the flotation, the face or coupon interest rate, the duration, the purpose of the issue, the date of sale, the price the bonds brought at the sale, the net yield at this price, the name of the purchaser, and, when possible, the basis price or net yield that the bonds brought when retailed. Every one of these facts is of prime importance in gauging the price to pay for municipals, for one should never, or almost never, bid with a first thought on competitive bids, but rather with heed first to the price that the market will bear, and next to the margin of profit that is acceptable under the conditions.

One house has just recompiled such a sales record, which consumed the time of two men for six months.

77. The application of these details of issue to prospective bidding becomes instinctive to a professional bond buyer. He will run through a few pages of proposals for bids and check off with almost unerring accuracy the cases in which no bids will be received. Usually he will err only when a local bank, for advertising or political purposes, bids above the market.

78. We will say that the rural County of X—— in New York State proposes at the

present time to issue $20,000 4¼% bonds maturing serially from date $2,000 each year. This item may not interest the experienced buyer. In the first place, the issue is a small one—hardly worth printing circulars for. Secondly, bonds in New York State may not be sold by municipalities below par: in this case a 4.25 per cent. basis. The best basis that a bond house can possibly expect to get for this bond in this market is 4.15 per cent. But the difference in a 4¼% bond of this duration between a 4.25 and a 4.15 per cent. basis is .474 or $4.74. This gross profit is or should be too narrow to draw out any bids.

79. Unintelligent Proposals for Municipals. Another aspect of the unintelligent offering of municipal loans is presented in the following illustration. Some time ago a municipality within gunshot of New York awarded an issue of bonds to various bidders at a price several hundred dollars less than the offer of another house for "all or none." Their action caused some comment at the time, although it was perfectly legal and apparently in good faith. In the light of that experience what shall we say of the stewardship of their officials when a year or so later the same mistake was repeated? The municipality made three awards at the sale, amounting to $153,262.76, whereas if the bonds had been awarded in one lot to the highest bidder the citizens would have received $153,589.96. Was not this $327.20 difference worth saving? A slightly different method of advertising the sale would have accomplished the result.

80. **Municipal Bond Bureaus.** I have already mentioned financial service bureaus that make relatively easy the statistical work of bond houses. There are at present two daily publications that keep bond concerns well posted on forthcoming municipal sales and the terms and forms in which proposals may or must be couched. They also publish lists of bidders at recent sales, with the prices obtained. Through the services of these bureaus the necessary data for intelligent buying of "legals" may be collected by merely clerical effort.

81. **General Market Municipals.** The problem of buying "general market" municipals is no such simple matter. In these bonds security may seldom be taken for granted. It *is* taken for granted much more generally than proper. The financial memory (to repeat) is proverbially short. Each generation forgets the fiscal follies and disasters of the preceding. History in finance makes so rapidly: When in 1839, during that long business depression in America that produced the first repudiation period, Baring Brothers of London inquired of Daniel

Webster concerning "the measure of security which the purchasers of bond issues by the states of the American Union would have for their investment," he wrote in reply:

"I believe there is no country upon earth—not even that of the injured creditor—in which such a proceeding (repudiation) would meet with less countenance or indulgence than it would receive from the great mass of American people."

Yet within two years Governor McNutt of Mississippi had recommended, and within three years the legislatures of Mississippi and Florida had voted the repudiation of nearly $9,000,000 of bonds.

82. **Municipal Defaults.** Did the default of these or of five other states in the forties deter European or American investors from further purchases? Not at all. Instead of using business sense, they continued trusting and buying, and losing. Nothing daunted they bought after the War, overlooking the war time default of three states; they bought in the eighties and nineties in spite of the repudiation of nine states in almost as many years. If the men of Lombard and Wall Streets and countless other bond buyers had taken the same pains in 1870 or thereafter to acquaint themselves with the factors of state credit, and of the errors of the legislatures and investing

public in the preceding generation, as they now do in the purchase of railroad securities, fewer bonds would have been floated at that time and less state paper would now repose in ancient pigeon holes.

83. The story of municipal loans is the same, only worse. How many men now active in the financial district realize that thirty years ago the Mississippi Valley gave up a long list of defaulting cities, among which were Duluth, Keokuk, McGregor, Quincy, Cairo, St. Joseph, Cape Girardeau, Lawrence, Topeka, Nebraska City, Little Rock, Helena in Arkansas, Memphis, Shreveport, New Orleans, Mobile and Houston? "Of one hundred counties, townships and cities issuing bonds in Missouri, nine-tenths have defaulted," says the North American Review in August, 1884.

84. The point is not, of course, that this country will ever again see a repetition of this wholesale breach of faith, but that the proposed debts of the weaker communities, such as rural counties, small towns and taxing districts, should receive the same expert investigation that is given the debts of private corporations. Although it is true that not for some years has an American municipality of importance failed to meet its valid obligations, nevertheless numbers of small communities in all parts of the country except New England

are at the present time failing to keep their pledges. In some cases it is through no obliquity on the part of the community; in most it is the result of official incompetency and political unwisdom; but whatever the causes, they should be studied by bond buyers that loans produced under improper conditions may be avoided.

85. There are millions of dollars of "Gravel Road" bonds issued under the Indiana Highway Act of 1905 (Chapter 167) that have hung in the balance between payment and non-payment for some years because they were issued under local and special authority. Originally declared unconstitutional, they have been fully validated by a review of the case in the Supreme Court of the State. But they illustrate the need of special fitness and professional training in the purchasing function, even in this day, and even for municipal loans.

86. What knowledge and experience may have been accumulated hitherto by the bond-houses has only recently found its way into print. The principles of municipal bond investment may be thoroughly explored, but only within the year have they been codified and published. We have at least reached this stage, that the bond buyers of the big New York banking houses will refuse municipal loans they believe unsound. They have com-

mon grounds for their faith. About three years ago a community that is almost within rifle shot of the city offered a loan in New York without success. It was finally placed with a Western house that has since failed. The bonds have defaulted, but nevertheless the community has just offered another loan. It would have been interesting to note what house would dare to purchase the bonds. It is reassuring to state that no bids were received.

87. The true financial competency of a community to issue, support and acquit bonded obligations is not so easy to ascertain as most people suppose. I venture the assertion that there are more bond men who can analyze an annual report of the United States Steel Corporation than who can analyze the financial statement of the City of New York. It is not important to seek the reason for this condition of things. But let us not underestimate the importance of the purchasing function of the bond houses as related to municipal issues. That the huge machinery of municipal debt creation and investment exchange runs so smoothly and with such exceedingly infrequent and unimportant casualties is sufficient testimony to the financial health of our bodies politic and of our investment houses.

CHAPTER IV.

BUYING RAILROAD BONDS.

88. In the preceding two chapters we discussed in as much detail as circumstances permitted the purchasing function of the bond houses, in its broad aspects of public and firm policy, and as related particularly to municipal issues. There remain to be considered the special principles that govern the buying of railroad and other private corporation bonds. This paper will be devoted to the railroad issues.

89. **Common Characteristics of Railroad and Municipal Bonds.** Railroad and municipal bond buying have some phases in common. Perhaps in both it is fair to say that an investigation of the ability of the obligor corporation to meet its engagements is not usually the *chief* consideration at the time of purchase. In other words the equities are *usually* sufficient to be accepted without that degree of exhaustive scrutiny which must be given to the equities of public service and industrial corporations. Secondly, the ultimate destination of a large part of both municipal and railroad debt is institutional, therefore the rapidity and capacity of absorption or "digestion" is relatively great, and these two types

BUYING RAILROAD BONDS 57

may be handled on a relatively narrow margin of profit. The margin for railroad bonds is not the scant three-quarters to one per cent. ($7.50 to $10.00 per $1,000 bond) we assumed for municipals of the "legal for savings banks" type, but let us say four or five per cent. Moreover, the market for railroad bonds (so large a part of which is listed) is self-regulating, even to a greater extent than the market for municipals, therefore the initial sale profit does not have to contain provision for subsequent cost of market support—a generally unconsidered expense of floating "specialty" corporation bonds by houses that take care of their customers.

90. A third point of likeness between these types is their division into two broad classes, the one in which security, in the ordinary sense, may be taken for granted almost absolutely, so that current money rates, and profits, determine the purchase, and the other in which the degree of security, marketability, etc., are determining price factors.

91. On the whole, however, the purchase of railroad bonds is more closely associated with that of corporations generally than with that of municipals, because of the very character of the debt and of the issuer.

92. **Railroad Bond Underwriting.** The buyer of railroad bonds of the prominent systems

faces a more difficult situation than the buyer of legal municipals. At present all the great American railroad systems are dominated by one or another of, say, half-a-dozen great banks or banking houses. It is therefore practically impossible for the "retail" bond houses (the kind described in these pages) to purchase large issues at first hand from these railroads, and therefore to obtain the profits indicated above. Indeed, in a recent interview, a prominent Wall Street corporation lawyer went so far as to declare that it was next to impossible for any corporation in this country to raise $10,000,000, outside the great banking groups provided the subscription would be inimical to the interest of any of them.

93. **Underwriting by Retail Houses.** However that may be, if a "retail" bond house chooses to specialize in the better railroad flotations it must align itself with those houses that are willing to act as secondary underwriters. It is then expected to participate in the sub-underwriting or actual purchase of the majority of issues fathered by the wholesale banker with which it is affiliated, almost irrespective of the quality and price of the issue, or the condition of the bond market. A railroad bond buyer needs tact as well as professional skill, to seize the horns of this dilemma, and keep his house in line for what

BUYING RAILROAD BONDS 59

is safe and profitable, without giving offense in declining what is either unsafe or unprofitable.

94. This dilemma is by no means imaginary or occasional; it is an ever present difficulty. On the one hand (as to safety), there is constant temptation to relax in critical caution and to follow the crowd into some new subscription to an uninvestigated security that promises profits overnight. If one could only know the amount, how startling would be the sum annually committed to subscription bond purchases for purely speculative objects, without any thought of regular merchandizing or investment, because of telephone tips, newspaper gossip, and neighborly hearsay! The bond houses make their share of these blind purchases.

95. If you ask for a copy of the mortgage it isn't yet ready for distribution, and you are a squeamish obstructionist. Yet one of the largest railroad systems in America, which issues many millions of bonds almost every year, through the usual New York banking channels, in the usual subscription manner, has had a net income for the past three years that has *averaged* less than 2¾ per cent. of the gross earnings! Another system, operating about 10,000 miles, during the year 1910 consumed 94½ per cent. of its gross earnings in

mandatory charges. During the year of the last panic almost 99 per cent. of all it earned was eaten up in charges. Yet instead of laying by for the next panic this road is again paying dividends on many millions of stock.

96. On the other hand (as to profits), current railroad subscription prices are put as high as the market will possibly bear,[1] and the eighth, quarter, half, or one per cent., or more, that goes to the retail houses for sub-underwriting from the big wholesalers is likely to be wiped out before the bonds are disposed of in such a sagging bond market as we have become thoroughly familiar with in the past two or three years.

97. **The Profits of Underwriting.** The public may not seem to be as directly concerned with the distribution, as with the total amount, of middlemen's profits when great railroad corporations borrow, but perhaps a warrantable interest can be made to appear; moreover, we are considering the work of the bond houses as such rather than the economics of finance, primarily. Well, let us assume for argument's sake that 6 points (or per cent. on par) represent the difference between what the railroad gets and the public pays at the initial sale, and that prior, or possibly subsequent, to public

---

[1] There has been one notable exception during the year 1911-12.

BUYING RAILROAD BONDS 61

flotation the big wholesaler assigns to three retail houses at 1½ points concession all bonds of the issue on hand soon after the public sale. The three retail houses in turn permit associate houses a discount of ¼ from established prices. These associate houses, however, act merely as brokers, whereas the three retailers mentioned have bought, paid for, and taken up the bonds or temporary certificates.

98. The question arises: Are the profits of the wholesalers, the secondary underwriters, and the brokers, respectively, proportionate to the services performed? Perhaps the interest of the brokers in the transaction may be omitted. They take no risk unless they choose to speculate for their own account; the bonds they buy are usually sold for the account and risk of others; therefore their profits are and should be nominal.

99. But should the wholesaler, who may own the bonds for a week, who is reasonably certain of their disposition, and has little direct future moral responsibility to the public, and who is under small direct selling expense, be entitled to four times the profits of the retailers on whom falls the real burden of selling and the real risk of loss through sagging prices? Whether the ratio is 4 to 1 or less, is it an evidence of sound economic conditions in any business when wholesale profits are greater than retail?

100. It may be argued that the great wholesalers have at command the immense capital necessary for the exploitation of steam transportation systems and are entitled to rewards commensurate with the advantage of their capitalistic entrenchment. There are dozens of retail houses that, under an unsubsidized banking system, and in "joint account," would be capable of handling the largest corporation loans that find ultimate placement on this side of the water—indeed the same houses that now are the immediate repositories of the loans until ultimate public absorption. Their federated banking resources are drawn upon almost as extensively, under present circumstances, as if the wholesalers were not involved.

101. **A Pennsylvania Railroad Flotation.** Two or three years ago when the Pennsylvania Railroad contemplated the issuance of a loan of many millions one of my good Boston friends (you may remember the newspaper story) offered with perfectly good financial warrant to bid for the bonds at public sale an amount in excess of the price reputed to have been arranged with the usual wholesale underwriters. This offer was not accepted, although he was courteously given interview with the president and other officials of the road. The publicity of the case made this much recog-

BUYING RAILROAD BONDS 63

nition advisable. The reason the offer was not accepted may perhaps be found in the statement of the corporation attorney, already quoted, concerning the impossibility of obtaining large loans without the acquiescence of financial autocracy.

102. Direct buying of railroad debts by the retail bond houses would tend, more than at present, to separate the banking interests from the proprietary interests and more closely to associate the banking interests with the investment interests,—both movements highly to be desired.

103. There is no opprobrium to be attached to the centralization of banking power. It is an inevitable phase of the industrial evolution of the past decade. It seems possible now that centralization may be followed by disintegration, but more probably by governmental regulation, built on any convenient legal principle that comes to hand when the time is ripe. I believe that, whatever the event, present artificial conditions cannot continue indefinitely, and that it will soon again be possible for the American bond houses to bid freely for the big railway loans as they now bid for legal municipals.

104. **Railroad Blanket Refunding Issues.** Even under present conditions the proper purchase of big railroad loans by the retail house

implies technical qualifications of a high order in the bond buyer. Opportunities (in street trading or otherwise) for the quick purchase of current issues at advantageous prices, demand a thorough working knowledge of all the big general and refunding issues, of which there are about forty—all but three or four of which are listed—and a knowledge of two or three dozen more of the important underlying and miscellaneous loans.

105. The preponderance of transactions in the refunding issues may not be appreciated by everybody. Convertibility (that is, marketability and hypothecary value), is of such tremendous advantage to certain types of investors, particularly institutions like national banks, that much higher prices may be obtained for issues of such magnitude and vogue as to assure a future fairly steady demand at current interest rates. Therefore, on the insistence of bankers, the railroads for the past decade have been satisfying their wants for new capital less and less by means of new first mortgage divisional issues, or the like, and more and more by new long term, virtually "open end" blanket mortgages covering the entire property and of sufficient amount, reserved in escrow, to retire at or before maturity the senior and miscellaneous issues of the road.

BUYING RAILROAD BONDS 65

106. The provisions of these blanket refunding mortgages are becoming standardized, to the great benefit of railroad finance. By gradual retirement of miscellaneous mortgages and issuance, in substitute, of escrow refunding bonds, not only is the tendency of railroad debt to become simplified and easier of appraisal, but to become more negotiable, as the escrow bonds of a refunding mortgage take the place of smaller loans. Hence the fact that there are now *outstanding* over $1,500,000,000 of these refunding bonds and forty or more issues a good railroad bond buyer should know in all essentials respecting security and price, gives us some notion of what is required of the buyer of the big issues. If a buyer has the responsibility of shaping up for the acceptance of his house a new issue, that is another matter. Railroad scholarship then is only a small part of his equipment. Even to skirt about his problem here would usurp space. But to resume:

107. The average profit in "turning over" these current issues is small—less even than in handling legal municipals—therefore a nice sense of market values and of the price trend is essential to success. Some of the best young aggressive houses on the Street have found it impossible to make enough money in current listed railroad issues to support a body

of bond salesmen. Ordinarily selling of this sort must be incidental to the distribution of other more profitable securities. Such profit as there is must be obtained very largely by a study of the course of bond prices in general and of the range of movement in the issue in question. It is easier to sell than to buy these bonds right. A table of monthly and annual price fluctuations of the securities (they are listed, remember) is an excellent index of relative cheapness and dearness. The number of sales on the Exchange and the volume of sales per annum, will also have significance.

108. One must not gain the impression from what has been said that the retail bond houses have no opportunity for direct and profitable relations with the railroads. The bonds they can buy and sell direct are usually of the second class. The big systems have subsidiaries which from time to time must put their name to paper, some of it very excellent indeed. Let us remember that the number of operating corporations with a mileage of 1,000 is about 50, but not very much over 50; that there are over 1,000 railways reporting to the Interstate Commerce Commission that have a mileage of under 250; that the number of carriers of the switching and terminal class is about 500; that the total number of industrial (as distinguished from commercial) railways is

BUYING RAILROAD BONDS 67

not far from 2,500, exceeding in mileage 25,000. Although not all these transportation agencies are direct obligors and emitting funded debt, nevertheless the sum of their annual output of bond issues is very large, and their debts are well worth the solicitation of banking houses that are equipped to handle them.

109. **Equipment Bonds.** Perhaps the most satisfactory form of railroad loan for these houses is equipment trust obligations. Inasmuch as the average life of the average issue is 5½ years the opportunities to profit from the reinvestment of funds thus placed is recurrent. It is the very general impression that "not a dollar of money invested in equipment bonds has ever been lost." This is not true. However, I have examined the history of every equipment issue of every road that has passed through reorganization or receivership since 1872, when equipment bonds were "invented," and state with conviction that the record and the present legal characteristics of the standard ten year serial equipment bond (of any of the three current types) is without parallel as respects security, except first mortgage gas bonds in metropolitan cities.

110. Equipment issues of some of the best systems are still to be bought direct by the bondhouse; also terminal, divisional and mis-. cellaneous issues. All classes of railroad bonds

of the smaller roads are to be had. The various kinds included here form the second division of railroad bonds corresponding, in some respects, as already stated, to the non-legal, or general market municipals.

111. Railroad Bond Investment Principles. The investment principles governing the purchase of the big refunding and of the miscellaneous railroad bonds are of course the same. In distinction from the principles of municipal bond investment, they are thoroughly established and recognized. Therefore an attempt to detail them is superfluous. Still a few comments of a general nature may not be amiss.

In approaching railroad investment study the general problems will be found to be definite in number, orderly in sequence, and now, with the jurisdiction of the Interstate Commerce Commission, of certain application at least to all roads that do an interstate business.

112. Proprietorship and Management. The first considerations, of Proprietorship and Management, are not the less important because irreducible to figures. The first thought of the investigator is, or should be, to the character and credit of the dominant proprietors. Financial heredity, in this matter, counts for more than most people realize. In Carl Snyder's excellent book on *American Railways as Investments,* 1907, he has this to say:

BUYING RAILROAD BONDS 69

"It is one of the most curious facts of railway history, but one exemplified fully enough, that careful and conservative conduct of a road tends in some sense to perpetuate itself. . . . . It is not for nothing that the Pennsylvania has never failed to pay a dividend for more than fifty years. It is not for nothing that roads like the Reading, the Erie, the Union Pacific, have been the footballs of stockjobbing speculators, and dishonest directors. The ownership of a road, the personnel of its management, may change absolutely, yet it is curious to note how amid all these changes its character for good or evil will sometimes survive."

It is a matter not of years but of decades to change the nature of a railroad. A knowledge of the conduct of a railroad stock on the Exchange, over a period of years, and of its dividend record, its history in receivership, will be a crude but reasonably safe guide to the general health of the road.

113. There is much to be learned from the history of any proprietorship or control. The holders of the underlying bonds of one of the Western systems have equities in earnings and securities that make the obligations appear of a very high type. But an analysis of the methods by which a comparatively small outlay of money obtained control of this property,

by means of a system of holding companies and stock pyramiding, will not reassure a careful bond buyer that his interest will be conserved. When only a few millions of cash were necessary to control a property bonded for some hundreds of millions, the market price of the best of its bonds was sure to suffer severely when it appeared that the system might not be able to meet all of its obligations.

114. Where there is a truly dominating interest, such as Moffat in the Denver, Northwestern, and Pacific; Flagler in the Florida East Coast; Atkinson in the Atlantic and Birmingham; Stilwell in the Kansas City, Mexico and Orient, or Hill in the Great Northern, the inevitable questions are: Is this a capable railroad man; is he constructive, and does he conserve minority interests; who are his bankers; in what other roads is he interested, and what other connections has he? The same questions hold good for a dominating group of men.

115. **Community of Interest.** No railroad development of the past ten years has greater significance to bond buyers than the general recognition of the necessity for that *entente cordiale* among the companies which arises from a "community of interest." The youngest of those who have interest in financial

BUYING RAILROAD BONDS 71

matters remembers the days of rate wars which drove so many roads into bankruptcy. When freight tariffs could not be maintained legally by competing carriers, through the agency of a pool, the desired result was obtained by the creation and recognition of a community of interest. The ownership by one road of the stock of another, with consequent dovetailing of directorates, led to amicable understanding and concert in action, when otherwise there might have been costly warfare.

116. But traffic alliances may exist without stock control by any party. Then the visible evidence of co-operation is to be found in the duplication of officers or directors. It is especially important that the smaller independent roads which do not originate sufficient traffic to make them self-sustaining should have the benefit of friendly connections with a powerful system to relieve them of the possibility of destructive competition. In the case of an aggressive independent road this possibility may be an impending probability. There are well known small roads that today have greater difficulty in maintaining their corporate independence against the aggressions of larger systems than they do in maintaining the standard of their service or the sufficiency of their earnings. The recognition of the community of railroad interest has done more than anything else, except the general development

of the country and of the railroads themselves, to place railroad finance upon its present stable footing.

117. Management. Management, as distinguished from proprietorship and control, may be looked upon as relating to the internal railroad policies governing the machinery of transportation. Subordinate in public interest to the financial heads and affiliations, the railroad managers and their work will be best known to the investigator by the records of physical and operating efficiency.

118. Physical Characteristics. The main physical characteristics to be subjected to the analytics of the bond buyer are the location of the railroad, the size or mileage, the character and condition of the equipment, and the operating efficiency. The uses to which information of this nature may be put will readily suggest themselves. It may not be so obvious, however, that a reliable source for this information exists. It is due to the uniform statistical requirements of the Interstate Commerce Commission that reliable data of this nature is available. Unfortunately their supervision does not extend back over a sufficient number of years to validate much historical comparison.

119. Earning Power and Capitalization. Besides the personnel and the physical characteristics, the studies of the railroad bond buyer will cover the company's earning power and the valuation and capitalization to which it is related. In these subjects also he is indebted to the Commission for thoroughly reliable and thoroughly detailed figures such as ordinarily may not be obtained regarding any other class of private corporations, and only with the greatest difficulty from municipal corporations. Earning power, or more broadly and technically the Income Account, and valuation, or the Capital Account, are elaborately and logically dissected by the Commission in such manner that no competent bond buyer can fail to comprehend the true financial condition of the obligor.

120. Publicity makes possible to any investor who is capable of it the same sort of *statistical* investigation that any banking house ought to give a railroad security it buys or recommends. But in want of ability, inclination or opportunity to study, the investor may accept the dictum of his bankers on railroad bonds, if ever, for a house that cannot give a competent opinion on an American railroad bond is not qualified to advise on any type of security. Not that such judgments are easily arrived at, but that the investment principles are of common acceptance and the material facts indisputable.

CHAPTER V.

BUYING CORPORATION BONDS.

121. Students can buy municipal or railroad bonds, but it takes business men to buy corporation bonds. In other words, we have now come to that point in the bond business where mere theory (with no reproach in the term) must be subordinated to special experience and native endowment to perform the purchasing function without inviting regrets. There is more here, also, of the spirit of the market place where Greek meets Greek in trade, and the firm with the shrewdest instinct for barter stands the best chance of success. Less capital is needed for corporation bond buying, for the average issue is smaller; therefore the field is open to a wider range of talent and a display of greater individual ingenuity in financing. But before considering the problems of this kind of buying we must come to some conclusion as to what are corporation bonds.

122. What Corporation Bonds Are. One who is at all sensitive to nice distinctions in terminology will object to a division of funded debt that excludes railroad loans from the class called corporation bonds. If railroad bonds are not corporation bonds none are. On the other hand, if one is going to be academic,

BUYING CORPORATION BONDS 75

cities and towns and some other municipalities are corporations — public corporations — and their bonds must therefore be corporation bonds.

123. Classification of Bonds. To show the difficulty of establishing a good nomenclature I give on the following page a rough classification of bonded debt according to the character of the issuer, or obligor.*

From this classification it will be seen there is no word or phrase, now current, that is properly descriptive of the transportation, public utility, industrial and miscellaneous issues that are not civil loans and are not railroad loans. Moreover, it will probably tax the ingenuity of any one to discover or coin such a word or phrase. Even as this classification stands, many will object to the separation of street railway and interurban railway securities and will wish to associate irrigation district bonds with municipals or quasi-municipals.

124. In want of logic a safe guide is custom, and custom loosely speaks of government, municipal, railroad, and corporation bonds, meaning by the last phrase, in a very general way, the issues that are classified in this

---

* There are three other logical and comprehensive classifications: according to the security for the bonds, according to the purpose or function of this issue, and according to conditions attending payment of interest and principal.

CLASSIFICATION OF BONDS.

- Civil Loans
  - Government Loans
    - United States Bonds
    - Bonds of Dependencies
    - Territorial Bonds
    - State Bonds
  - Municipal Loans
    - Municipals Proper
      - City Bonds
      - Bonds of Incorp. Towns
      - Bonds of Incorp. Villages
    - Quasi Municipals
      - County Bonds
      - Parish Bonds
      - Township Bonds
      - Borough Bonds
      - Precinct Bonds
      - Assessment Bonds, i. e., Bonds of Tax Districts

- Corporation Loans
  - Transportation Bonds
    - Railroad Bonds
    - Steamship Bonds
    - Ferry Bonds
    - Express Co. Bonds
    - Interurban Railway B'ds
  - Public Utility Bonds
    - Street Railway Bonds
    - Gas Bonds
    - Electric Light Bonds
    - Water Bonds
    - Water Power Bonds
    - Telephone Bonds
  - Industrial and Miscellaneous Bonds
    - Reclamation Issues
      - Irrigation Bonds
        - Irrigation District Bonds
        - Carey Act Bonds
        - Bonds of Private Projects
      - Levee Bonds
      - Drainage Bonds
    - Timber Land Bonds
    - Real Estate Bonds
    - Mining Company Bonds

scheme below railroad bonds. Hence the caption of this article, although it contradicts the very classification in question.

125. Nothing more than a glance at the classification is necessary to establish in any one's mind the fact that the professional bond buyer faces more difficult and varied problems in this type than in any of the security types we have dealt with previously. It will be conceded at sight that in corporation bonds security is first, last, and always the prime consideration. Literally, on the fingers of two hands may be counted the bonds of which the security may be taken for granted, relatively speaking, and attention be devoted to the intensity of the investment demand and future advantages from the fiscal relationship.

126. **Corporation Bond Investment Principles.** If security is the main problem and so many very unlike species come under the genus corporation bonds, it is correspondingly difficult to sum up the investment principles governing their purchase. This much may be said at the outset: to buy intelligently any type of corporation bond one must know the kind of business the corporation is engaged in.

127. **Knowing the Business of the Corporation.** If a house is considering the bonds of an independent telephone company in Kansas or Nebraska, it is not sufficient to analyze with

the utmost care the credit and earning power of this company, and the general physical efficiency of its plant; it is necessary to study the character of Western telephony as related to Western social conditions, and the place of this company's particular kind of service in the scheme of telephonic communication the country over; it is necessary to come to some conclusion as to the likelihood of later cordial affiliation with some large system with long-distance, interstate activities; it is necessary to understand the policy of the Bell system and the Bell attitude toward independents in general. In a word, one must learn the telephone business.

128. **Water Companies.** It is surprising how much material for thoroughly practical individualistic study is offered in any of the fields of commercial endeavor covered by the obligations that have been classified. Water companies, perhaps, operate under conditions that approximate simplicity and uniformity more closely than most other obligors of corporation bonds. Yet the amount of labor that certain bond houses have put into purely statistical study of these companies is incredible. Have you, for instance, any notion as to whether there is a known relation between the per capita debt of these companies and the size of the community served? Or what propor-

tion of gross earnings is properly applicable for maintenance and renewals in this as compared with other public utility corporations?

129. **Gas Companies.** The operation of gas companies also seems fairly simple; that is, so far as manufacturing and distribution problems have any direct relation to investment in gas bonds. Yet we must consider, must we not, what danger manufacturing plants run of being supplanted by the discovery of new sources of natural gas, which can be piped a great distance? We must know whether electricity threatens to overthrow gas as an illuminant, as gas to a large extent took the place of oil, and oil of candles. To know this we must follow the history of improvements in gas and electric lighting to Welsbach and tungsten incandescence. If gas is being supplanted to any appreciable degree we must appraise the other outlets for its consumption, as heat and power. Then there is the danger of reduction in rates. As rates have been reduced in the past, have earnings decreased or has growth in per capita use and in population, and has the utilization or residuals offset the decline in price? Is there any relation between equitable rates and the population served? To know gas bonds, then, one must know something more than the mere outlines of the gas business.

130. Perhaps it is more evident now than in the earlier papers of this series what estimable service may be rendered a banking house by a competent statistical force in gathering material which shall be the basis of sound business judgments. Unfortunately, but quite naturally, most material that is gathered in this way never appears in print. It is personal or firm property and is too valuable to be given away.

131. **Street Railways.** A representative of one of the big down-town banks came to me recently to be directed to a trustworthy source of printed information concerning street railways, by means of which to learn the essentials of security in street railway stocks and bonds. I gave him what platitudes I had written on the subject and all the others I knew about, but told him his quest was hopeless; he would have to learn street railroading to be sure of his ground. What he wanted was not for publication.

132. **The Income of Public Service Corporations.** Public institutions can afford to be less niggardly of their data. An earnest of what may be done in a statistical way that is of immense practical value to banking houses and investors is furnished by the Tuck School of Finance, Dartmouth College. Prof. W. H. Lyon is setting several of the Tuck School

BUYING CORPORATION BONDS 81

men at work on theses that are designed to show the effect of changing commercial and financial conditions on the earning power of various industries. Something distinctive and valuable will be gained, when we know what effect a short panic or a longer commercial depression has on the gross and net income of all the leading types of public service corporations.

133. The point of all this, so far as it concerns the public, is to know what houses do and what houses do not identify with themselves engineers and other specialists competent to pass upon the technical problems that each class of bonds gives rise to. But the public doesn't know and cannot know. All the public can do is to patronize the houses that among the fraternity have the reputation for technical competence. Is it strange that as a rule the same houses that are considered technically competent have a reputation for conservatism—much abused word? Banking houses, like servants, have "characters," and there isn't much disagreement in the profession as to which are good, which bad, and which indifferent.

134. **Bond Houses as Specialists.** Some houses make a specialty of one type of bond: Electric light and power, water, real estate, or it may be irrigation. In this case it is quite

82 BUYING CORPORATION BONDS

probable that they are reconstructors, operators, and managers in their specialty, and therefore competent appraisers of property values. Per contra, the presumption is that because of their very specialization they may be weak in banking experience, and in the many excellent business qualities that characterize the better American bond house. Yet all bond men will recall one or two notable exceptions to both rules.

135. The Newness of Corporation Bonds. The most eminent characteristic of corporation bond dealings is the newness of them. Take up a copy of "Poor's Industrial Manual" and open at random. The chances are that five times running your eye will light on bond issues dated within ten years—even apart from refunding loans. This newness, rather than insufficient earning power, is the source of much public aloofness from corporation loans. There is basis for the feeling. Water supply is immemorial; the gas business nearly a century old; but street and interurban railroading, electric lighting, hydro-electric service, telephony and irrigation have not attained their majority. Furthermore, although the steamship business is of long standing, and the lumber business and real estate operations are antediluvian in origin, the principles of bond investment have been commonly applied to them only very recently. It takes years to establish speculative and investment principles on a basis of experience that will warrant the invitation of cautious, responsible funds.

136. Time will remedy youthfulness; and in any case youthfulness is not quite the cardinal difficulty, but inexperience. Types of business service that are common to all communities, particularly perhaps to Eastern communities and to cities, generally attain their experience most rapidly. They become "standardized." Kinds of service that are universally required in settled communities—water, light, power, and communication—are most rapidly attaining fiscal maturity. Therefore public utility bonds have until very recently held a rank in common esteem midway between railroad and the "industrial and miscellaneous" loans.

137. **Industrial Issues.** One of the big questions that the buyer for the bond house must decide is whether his firm shall lend its name to any industrial issues. It is a question of policy rather than of relative security. The public utility field, intrinsically, is safer because earnings are more definitely predicable. But the competition for good public utility bonds is so keen, and for good industrials so slight, that it is easier to find loans of the latter type that have the necessary intrinsic merit.

138. **The Competition for Public Utility Bonds.** I say the competition for public utilities, i. e., public service corporation bonds, is keen. In the first chapter I said that the competition among promoters to obtain placement for their loans was keen. The two statements are not contradictory. So far as offerings by promoters are concerned, they are innumerable. Many of them have merit. But the bond buyer has not only merit to consider but the policy of the firm and the character of the firm's clientele. To get a loan that is both good in itself and suitable to the nature of the demand—that is the difficulty. Many propositions are offered, but few are chosen. Hence a bond house that will handle corporation loans cannot reach any great distributive power without maintaining at least one competent investigator or buyer on the road. Sometimes this man is an engineer. At others he is a member of the firm. In either case the judgment of the man in the field looking for possible corporations and loans will be supplemented by others with different qualifications: those who look at the purchase from a different angle.

139. In the engineer's mind will be emphasized the value of the physical properties, the strategy of their location, and the future duration of their serviceableness pitted against

wear and tear, improvements and new inventions. The auditor will seek to read from the company's books an immaterial expression of the company's character, the truth concerning its earning power, and the uses to which the earnings have been put. The statistical expert will interpret the report of engineer and auditor in terms with investment meanings. The sales manager will consider the attractiveness of the security thus interpreted to the kind of investment demand the firm is prepared to satisfy. The bankers themselves, fully apprised by these specialists of the various qualities of the proposed issue, will determine the feasibility of "carrying" the securities under the present condition of the firm's credit at the banks, and the condition of credit in general.

140. **The Preference for Public Utilities.** The feeling against industrial loans is not so strong as it was five years ago, or three years ago. There are several reasons. The growth of the scientific spirit in business increases the stability of the large industrial corporations that seek to emit funded debt through banking channels. The decreased purchasing power of money stimulates interest in loans of higher yield than offered by public service bonds. The very difficulty of the public service purchase problem and the greater profits in indus-

trial flotations, influence the bond houses to attempt to widen the legitimate investment interest of their patrons by a campaign of education regarding what is essential and what is desirable in investments.

141. If any readers of this book are skeptical regarding the reputed profits of municipal and railroad bond selling, it must be because they do not believe business can be successfully conducted on such narrow margins as these pages have declared. They overlook two things: the self-supporting nature of the goods dealt in, and the consequent immense volume of business done per unit of capital. Incredulity is misplaced. If there has been any error it has been in overstating, not understating the profits.

142. **The Profit in Corporation Bonds.** But when we come to corporation bonds it is another story. The gross profit in corporation bond selling is very substantial. It will run from 5 to 15 per cent; and if the loans are wisely chosen this will be only a part of the ultimate profit, for it is indeed a fairly easily sold loan that will be bought without a substantial bonus of stock that eventually should pay handsome dividends.

143. There is no need of concealment or apology for these profits. There is no material here for the over-acute critic with senses whet-

ted for evil in anything that comes out of Wall Street.

144. No firm or group of firms has a monopoly of the corporation bond business. The market for the loans is perfectly free. The capital requirements of few companies in the country are too heavy for satisfaction by any one of many banking houses. In so far at least as public service corporations are concerned, the offerings of thoroughly meritorious issues are not so numerous that any have to go begging from saturation of the investment markets. Therefore the price of, or profits from, handling corporation loans is adjusted to the cost of distribution.

145. **Costly Distribution.** If there is any good basis at all for criticism of the gross profit in distribution—and maybe there is—it lies not in the residual profits that remain with the retail bond houses, but in the unscientific, costly method of distribution. Let me repeat an important statement made previously: the science of bond buying has developed more rapidly than the science of bond selling, or distribution. The cost of distribution, and possible remedies, belong more properly to another chapter. If this undue cost could be ascertained and subtracted from the gross profit the resulting net would appear not more than a fair reward for the fiscal service rendered.

146. Construction Propositions. Properties that are in the construction stage do not meet with banking favor. They are speculations pure and simple, and properly require speculative financing, with which the bond houses in their proper functions have nothing to do.

147. Demonstrated plant value and demonstrated earning power are pre-requisites of an investment interest. When a company doing a kind of business that the public knows something about has this value and earning power but needs to enlarge its facilities more rapidly than it can pay for out of surplus income, its natural recourse is the bond house. In this case the service of the house is principally, if not solely, fiscal, and its compensation for financing the needed enlargements may come largely, if not wholly, from the bond selling profits.

148. This country is developing too rapidly, however, for normal business growth by accretion alone. Small enterprises are forced into large or driven to the wall. Industries here, there, and everywhere engulf or are engulfed. Distances and time are disregarded in the struggle for control.

149. The Bond Houses as Reorganizers. The bond houses, therefore, are receiving more and more frequent appeals to finance plans of amalgamation and reorganization. This fiscal service is more speculative than the former, and requires for satisfactory results a higher degree of administrative capacity. Henceforth no house may expect to become identified in a large way with corporation finance that is not equipped to direct in part the policies of the companies it assists. As time goes on the line of separation will disappear between the engineering corporations with banking subsidiaries having security outlets and the banking houses with engineering and operating departments.

150 In line with this thought there is no reason why a firm that adheres most scrupulously to investment ideals should not promote and support through the construction stage any enterprise the firm is technically qualified to further, provided it does not put out securities to the public until they are ripe. It will be seen, however, that to the extent firms pursue this policy they are disqualifying themselves, as firms, from developing the purely banking function; and the banking function is more closely kin to their main business—the selling of investment bonds.

151. Although this mutual attraction of the banking and operating elements of modern industry may cause misgivings on the part of those purists who, if they could, would insist at all costs on the distinction between investment aloofness and speculative participation

in active affairs, nevertheless it may prove the best thing that could happen to business generally. A smaller percentage of bond houses, perhaps, may close a quarter century of honorable business without loss to any client, but a larger percentage of those who entrust their funds to corporate enterprise may receive commensurate returns.

CHAPTER VI.

THE ADVISORY FUNCTION.

152. **Advising a Woman.** I was once associated with "the buying side" of a banking house that is widely known for the uprightness of its dealings with clients. A lady unknown to us came into the office one day bent on buying a certain listed industrial preferred stock, but reluctant to do so without first talking the matter over. In the absence of the sales manager I discussed with her the merits of this stock, but advised her to purchase, in preference, the best unlisted public utility bond we then had to offer. The income from these two investments was practically the same— something over five per cent., but the security for the bond would be considered by most people superior. At least the marketable value would be more stable, and also the periodicity and amount of the income, presumably. Furthermore (without meaning to reflect on the highly valuable services of the stock exchanges) it is my experience that the evil genius of widely posted quotations has even a more baneful effect on women than on men.

153. At this point in the interview the sales manager appeared, and after explanations all round asked me in the presence of the pros-

pective customer if I didn't think a certain underlying divisional railroad issue more suitable for her. To be sure. But I knew that it would be impossible to sell her any of these, quite irrespective of the fact that there was no profit in them to speak of, for a scant 4 per cent. has no attractions to people who look takingly at high-yield industrial preferred stocks.

So we—or rather the manager—did as one would like to be done by, hewed square to the line, stated unwelcome investment truths, gave entirely disinterested advice, and the lady went elsewhere to make her purchase, whatever it may have been, evidently deficient in acquaintance with human nature as well as with investments.

154. The Ethics of Salesmanship. It would be idle to affirm that an incident like this illustrates the general temper of bond salesmanship. The millennium has not yet come to the security houses, nor have many of them more than bowing acquaintance with the golden rule. They are not in business to save a client in spite of himself or herself. But the most successful bond salesman I know is unequivocally honest in the advice he gives his customers, and of the many salesmen who have worked with me and under me I have never known one who I believe would deliberately play upon the business ignorance of women or other dependent persons.

155. Perhaps the close of the preceding sentence looks like an anti-climax; but is it? In how many lines of business is there a distinct, recognized ethical code that transcends the law and even the broader consideration of business expediency? One looks to some of the professions, like medicine, to find an analogy. This thought leads to another that I like to emphasize as frequently as may be. When the bond business is conducted as efficiently as possible from the standpoint of the investor, when the advisory function is developed to its proper proportions, the bond business has become a profession. To the extent that now a bond house or its traveling representatives can be consulted as a man consults his physician or his attorney, relying not altogether on the personal integrity of his consultee (to coin a word), but also on the recognized code of ethics in the fraternity—to that extent the bond business has become a profession entitled to the respect and confidence we have for and in professional men who value service above compensation.

156. **Financial Jackals.** Would that it were not necessary, in fidelity to truth, to note exceptions. Nevertheless, I can now recall only one New York bond house, and only one

Boston house, that I have reason to believe, from occasional contact, to be virtually wanting in ordinary business integrity. There may well be others, for my experience is limited. However, is this testimony not a little out of the ordinary?

157. The time was when so much could not be said for the security bankers. Not very many years ago there was a house of almost national reputation that, taken out of the hands of its founder but carried on in his name, laid waste many a fortune. The plundering was open and shameless. The piratical character of the salesmanship was even the subject of jest in doggerel verse, circulated from the home office among the employees.

158. I remember calling in those times on a lady who was among the prominent bond-buyers of Salem. One day she excused herself from doing business with me on the ground that she had just sold to a salesman of this house an old, seasoned, underlying railroad 5 per cent. bond at par, in exchange for the bond (sold at a discount) of a railroad in New Mexico, on which I knew the ties were never laid. She was felicitating herself on this exchange because her old bond, when due, would be worth only par, the salesman said, and he very generously offered to pay her the

THE ADVISORY FUNCTION 95

amount now, in advance of maturity, and not only that, but he was to sell her another 5 per cent. railroad bond, a first mortgage railroad bond, too, for which she would have to pay only $950. So she was to gain $50.

159. That is the sad side of bond selling. I tried very hard in the days of my apprenticeship to do business with the widow of a Boston physician. Her husband had left her a modest house with its furnishings, and $20,000 of life insurance. The life insurance she could have lived on very nicely in well-chosen, well-scattered 5 per cent. bonds. The money finally went into 9 per cent. California oil bonds. She liked my appearance, she said, and would like to do business with me. But why should she buy 5 per cent. bonds when she could buy 9 per cent. bonds at the same price? May that oil company prosper! In this case no bond house was to blame.

160. Naturally, the damage done legitimate bond selling by financial jackals is very great. Every sales manager, even of the most favorably known houses, realizes how much business is lost because of them. Let a bond man leave the beaten paths for a day, even in such a "well-combed" State as Connecticut, and he will be liable to a greeting that should have been given his more successful swindling predecessor, who called with worthless stock

for sale. How few, relatively speaking, are the places whence he will be turned away because of regretted visitations from his competitors in the bond business!

161. Ethically, the advice of the bond houses is excellent, whether coming direct from the office or through salesmen. Technically, its value is highly variable in this country, due to the fact that our financial houses are still, primarily, merchants of securities rather than counselors. It is hard to be fair as between two securities carrying very unequal profits. That is one reason why, in the previous chapter I intimated that the merging of banking and operating functions in a bond house has its drawbacks. It impairs the value of the advisory function.

162. As merchants, rather than counselors, the major effort is still to "move the goods," and, as I have stated in the introduction to "The Principles of Bond Investment," the salesman goes upon the road trained in address, primed with the latest gossip of new ore-bodies and melon-cutting, and with the talking points of his leading bonds—the bonds he wants the most to sell,—really sincere and frank in interpreting the information on his circulars, but for the most part inconsiderate of the wants of his clients, quite unable to comprehend or explain the essential invest-

ment qualities in the bonds he offers—unable, for instance, to tell whether there is a difference between a bond and a note, or between a car-trust certificate and an equipment bond. Salesmanship, so represented, is not a profession but a trade. It will be surprising if a decade does not improve this condition of things. Business, in self-interest, is becoming reconciled to scientific management. Some day, in self-interest, it will become reconciled to scientific salesmanship.

163. **English Selling Methods.** Capital, in England, may not, with propriety, seek its requirements from strangers. Introductions are necessary for immediate contact. The customary communication with private persons is through solicitors or through brokers; with institutions like insurance companies it is through company brokers. It is not good form, in turn, for the brokers to advertise, or to circularize any except people to whom they are known in a personal way. The distinction between banking and brokerage houses is carefully preserved, and business regulations, generally, tend to recognize the difference between merchants of securities and counsellors regarding their sale. Therefore, it is far more difficult to rob the unsophisticated part of the British public than Americans who are unfamiliar with securities.

164. Just as Easterners believe that Western business men more highly esteem optimism and debonair aggressiveness as business virtues, than accuracy and unbiassed judgment, so the British rightly regard us as a nation of special pleaders in matters of industry.

165. **Financial Advisory Systems.** Nevertheless, the change in this respect that has taken place among us during the past decade has been very remarkable indeed. In response to a real demand a number of investment advisory systems have sprung up, which, with nothing but financial information for sale, endeavor to work with bond houses and other banking institutions in disseminating reliable news and opinions. I have already referred to some of these advisory systems in mentioning the statistical helps that are available to the professional buyers in bond houses. However, in our country every now and again one of these systems will lapse from its good calling to deal in securities, directly and frankly, or by subterfuge. It is then in the category of a physician who prescribes to a patient nostrums in which he has a pecuniary interest. The time will come when such a state of things will be as inconceivable in securities as in medicine. Surely, it is very short-sighted policy thus to invite distrust and disrepute from the public at large, as well as to alienate

THE ADVISORY FUNCTION 99

the bond houses which are still the principal sustenance of these systems.

166. The greatest single influence affecting security purchases in America is probably the press in its narrative and editorial capacity. The next greatest influence, perhaps, is the American custom of personal solicitation by security salesmen. Solicitation is the apt word—unfortunately shall we say? The third influence may be the press in its advertising capacity.

167. **Bond Advertising.** Until very recently there were only two kinds of advertising a kid glove bond house might do. The first was to insert a "card" with the firm name (and membership maybe), and with the briefest possible statement of the various banking functions. To this might be added, parenthetically as it were, the fact that securities were bought and sold—of course for the accommodation of clients. The second was to print a broadside, offering an issue of bonds with particulars regarding the form, interest rate, price, duration, etc., but, for the sake of dignity, with all arguments to prove the issue a desirable investment couched in a letter purporting to come from the president of the obligor company.

168. **General Publicity.** Both of these forms of advertising are useful and proper.

100 THE ADVISORY FUNCTION

The cost of the first must be charged to "General Publicity," a most unsatisfactory, if necessary, account. The cost of the second may be charged to the account of a definite series of transactions, namely, the purchase and subsequent sale of the issue advertised; but very much less business than most people suppose directly results from this kind of expenditure. It is now not unusual for a bond house to make such a public offering and calmly state at the bottom that all the bonds are sold and the advertisement is "merely a matter of record." But more commonly, if the issue is of such a nature as to sell itself out of the hands of the underwriters into the hands of the secondary purchasers, the public offering is supposed to be good for a time from 5 minutes to a day after the opening of the books for orders.

169. **Advertising Investment Principles.** A third, more recent form of advertisement, deserves all the encouragement in resultant business that it can get, for when properly conducted it is a very influential expression of the bond houses in their advisory capacity. This form discusses the nature and the essential elements of investment with the application of this nature and these elements to the needs of some class of investors or to the characteristics of some bond issue. A glance at the financial page of the principal New York

THE ADVISORY FUNCTION 101

daily papers will recall just which high-grade houses use this method of advertisement, and how "Advisory advertisment" ought to pay best. Perhaps it does, because it gives a reader the impression that the signatory house has a full sense of its duty as counsellor of investments.

170. It is not easy to write such advertisements. Any series of notices on the same theme becomes monotonous after a while. Deliberate repetition is less hum-drum than unskilful variation. Space is costly, and nothing but broad generalization is possible in two inches of single column. But if advertisements are meant to be read, this third class is useful as well as significant of a growing professional sense among the bond houses.

171. **Special Circulars.** Less recent in origin and of greater vogue is the special circular containing investment truths. Usually it *is* truth, if not wholly sincere. One should not expect too much, and the difference between truthfulness and entire sincerity is the difference between the best spirit in modern business and the spirit of the millennium. In other words, the statements on the bond house circular are facts. They can be relied on. They are as exact as brains and care can make them. What one must look twice for, however, are the omissions. These remarks apply not only to

the brochures on general investment topics, but to the circular offerings as well.

172. Investment by Correspondence. Lastly, the bond houses have opportunity to direct investments wisely by means of correspondence. Very little of this correspondence originates with the investor. Most of it is the "confirmation" in writing of offers made by salesmen. The confirmation is the excuse for a more direct and personal presentation of the merits of the issue or issues that have been offered. Not being of public knowledge it is more likely to express the true character of the house.

173. If, therefore, you wish to test the quality of half-a-dozen banking houses, send each of them a letter of the following purport: "Brown, Jones & Robinson.

Gentlemen:—My husband has recently died leaving me with $25,000 which is distributed in the savings banks of the neighborhood. Would you advise that I keep some or all of it there, or put it into bonds or mortgages? If in bonds, what kind of bonds should I buy, and have you any to suggest.

Thanking you for your attention, etc."

The gentle feminine reader will do well to insert some little fib about being too delicate to receive strangers, or in twenty-four hours the neighborhood will think she has advertised for another husband.

Seriously, it is no fault to see business large in such a letter and to set hot foot after it, but whether reply is first by letter, as it should be, or by visitation, a keen person will appreciate which banking houses are true to their proper advisory function and which are mere pedlers of paper.

CHAPTER VII.

THE PROTECTIVE AND BANKING FUNCTIONS.

174. The Mercantile vs. the Protective Policy. The work of the bond house, as trustee for its clients, is closely associated with its advisory function, which we have just considered. Again attention is called to the alternatives it faces. It may have inherited and accepted the purely mercantile policy. It may consider itself merely a merchant of securities, with cessation of all responsibility to its customers on fulfillment of the selling contract, written or implied. Or on the other hand it may assume the protective function without criticism or demur from any source, and feel a moral responsibility concerning every bond it has placed with persons or investment institutions. Of course it will never, under any circumstances, feel bound, except as a matter of policy, to make good any kind of loss, that ensues from issues it has handled that originally were investigated and bought by brokers or other banking houses; nor will it feel bound with respect to persons or institutions that have made their purchases of its own specialties indirectly, through other

THE BANKING FUNCTION 105

houses. Indeed, some bond houses will deal on the street and among houses of other cities in securities they would not offer to clients.

175. The Spirit of Trusteeship. The sense of obligation, the spirit of "trusteeship" may find expression in a binding contract, or in a deliberately advertised policy, or it may be known only when put to the test of financial trouble.

176. Bond Guaranty. One cannot with good grace criticize the spirit of obligation that expresses itself in a guaranty of bond issues, whether this guaranty is of a banking house direct, as rarely, or of a trust company, or of a guaranty company. Such criticism, moreover, is likely to meet with little sympathy in most quarters. The conspicuous success of certain guaranty companies will rise up and overshadow the numerous obscure failures. Guaranties can be made sound. There is no doubt of that. They have been made sound in notable instances. But there are certain postulates to soundness that seem to preclude the guaranty principle from being *generally* sound. The securities guaranteed must be of a high order of safety in themselves, and the guarantor company must have assets far in excess of any probable demand of contingent liabilities. But securities of the sort that are appropriately guaranteed hardly need the pro-

106 THE PROTECTIVE FUNCTION

tection, and directly or indirectly, a part of the profits from their sales must, through long years go to the upbuilding of the equity in assets that gives the guaranty value.

177. Furthermore, the principle back of the guaranty is an insurance principle, not an investment principle. Insurance must be paid for. It is paid for by the insured. The insured has to pay not only for indemnity but for the cost of *clearing* the insurance, i. e., the guaranty company's operations.

178. **The Cost of the Guaranty.** The intelligent investor, who can choose a safe investment, yet pays for a guaranty, assumes the burden of the unintelligent investor. What is the price? Well, in real estate mortgages, where the guaranty principle has been developed most fully, the customary cost to the intelligent investors of his weaker brethren's liabilities of loss equals one-ninth of his income; rather costly charity, is it not? It is only fair, however, to state that this one-ninth covers not only the cost of *certainty* of payment, but the cost of *promptness* of payment, and relief from all details of investment management.

179. In bonds, this one-ninth (assuming one-ninth of income to be the cost) could not be made to cover *promptness* and *relief from details,* as well as *certainty,* because in bonds the former two of these three investment elements

THE BANKING FUNCTION 107

exist in a far higher degree and are part compensation for a possible less income, other things being equal.

180. It is to be observed, and quite naturally enough—that the guaranty is more commonly used to reinforce real estate bonds than any other kind; and of real estate bonds, those secured by farm mortgages. Farm mortgage real estate bonds are now invading the East as never before. One or two well-known Wall Street houses built up their business on this paper in days gone by. But now Tom, Dick and Harry are in the field selling securities that have been dug up and guaranteed in Texas and Oklahoma by local trust and mortgage companies.

181. Oklahoma, by the way, has had to learn by costly experience the insurance principle that underlies the guaranty. It is to be questioned whether, in the long run, bond guaranties will prove any more economically sound than bank deposit guaranties, in Oklahoma or anywhere else. One must not forget that there is a distinct difference between the distribution of risk, as in fire and life insurance, where accidents and loss are inevitable, unforeseeable, and in investment where one can choose the degree of risk he is willing to assume.

182. **The Protective Function Applied to**

108 THE PROTECTIVE FUNCTION

Marketability. The protective function, as an advertised moral obligation, is usually confined to matters of negotiability. It is not good form and it certainly would be poor business to advertise that one would make good all losses due to suspension of interest or principal payments. A house that will create a market for its issues has burden enough to carry to fulfill its pledge. The truth of this has been strikingly evident these past three years of declining bond prices. Nevertheless, in the face of the decline the policy of creating a market for "specialties" is steadily growing and advertisements to this effect are coming to be looked upon as a matter of course.

183. The amount of "protection" afforded by the creation of a specialty market depends, of course, upon the price at which a bond house is willing to buy back the issues it has fathered. We are likely to forget that the "security" of a bond is a very complex thing. Security of principal and security of interest, for example, are, or may be, quite distinct and almost unrelated investment elements. This fact is most appreciable in income bonds. Likewise security of principal, as determined by the probability of the payment of the face of the bond at maturity, and security of principal as determined by the probability of conversion in cash without loss during the life of the loan

THE BANKING FUNCTION 109

are two distinct and almost unrelated investment elements.

184. To make practical application of this thought to the bond business,—I have much greater confidence that New York City 4½'s of 1956 will be paid when due than I have that the Blank Electric Company First Mortgage 5's of 1949 will be redeemed at maturity. But if I may need to cash my investment five years from now I have greater confidence that Brown, Jones & Robinson will pay me within two points of what the Blank Electric 5's cost than that the open market for New York City 4½'s of 1956 will be within two points of the present market. Thus by exercising the protective function marketwise Brown, Jones & Robinson are strengthening the security-in-liquidation of my investment quite apart from security-in-redemption.

185. **The Cost to Clients of Artificial Marketability.** In the previous paragraph a two point difference was suggested as a possible "expectation of loss" due to liquidation of specialties, under normal conditions when the specialties were protected by the sponsoring bond house. I think that two points is a fair figure. If there has been a substantial appreciation in any given bond these may be no loss but in fact a gain. Conversely if the whole bond market is "off" the loss in liquidation

110 THE PROTECTIVE FUNCTION

may be more than two points. If the issue has become "digested" like the Aurora, Elgin and Chicago First 5's, the Union Electric Light and Power Co. (St. Louis) First 5's or the Milwaukee Gas Co. First 4's, then the margin between selling price and subsequent buying price will be narrower than if the issuing house has still a large unsold block on its hands.

186. As you stop to think of it, what a remarkable situation you face when a body of merchants (security merchants) have so developed the paternalistic function that they can adopt a policy of buying back at a fair price what they have once sold you, after years of alien ownership. Fortunately securities, like wine and friends do not become second hand and are likely to improve with age.

187. **Bonds as Collateral.** No other type of investment security has developed this kind of convertibility to such an extent as bonds. The loan value of bonds exceeds that of *all* other kinds of pure investment. As I have said previously, the highly desirable hypothecary value of bonds is largely overlooked by professional men who seek a channel for their surplus; it is overlooked by most people who have little dealing with banks. The great system of American bond houses is built and financed on the superior hypothecary value of bonds.

THE BANKING FUNCTION 111

188. Then do I make myself clear when I say that the bond houses, in protecting to the full the convertibility, or negotiability, of their securities, stand ready to act in the double capacity of buyers and bankers? To accommodate you, so that you need not lose money, they will buy of you or loan to you.

189. **The Banking Function of Bond Houses.** This, therefore, is the genesis of the banking function, to protect clients who need only temporary realization on their securities. But the bond houses are fully equipped with men, methods, and machinery, to say nothing of temper, for the conduct of any sort of banking, in so far as it relates to the personal affairs of their clients. They do not make good commercial banks to be sure; they are not good banks of discount; but as banks of deposit, for checking accounts, or for savings or for personal loans, they do as well as any, and I have no question the good ones are as safe as the average "institutional" bank, if not safer.

190. **The Cost to Bond Houses of Artificial Marketability.** It is evident that there is no profit in repurchasing bonds to protect clients. Two points is a low cost of liquidation. If five to fifteen points, plus a stock bonus, represents the initial selling cost plus a fair profit, two points cannot represent any profit over the cost of a second sale of inactive securities,

even conceding that the selling cost becomes less as the issue becomes assimilated and the "campaign of education" begins to bring its results. Moreover, in the majority of cases the resale of the old security with a two point gross profit prevents the initial sale of a like "undigested" security with its five to fifteen point profit.

191. If, on the other hand, we deal in a bond that will resell itself, then the repurchase price will not be a fixed difference from the original sale price but will be determined by the public market. Therefore, although the cost to the bond house of finding a second purchaser will be nominal, its profit will also be purely nominal because it must bid for the bond approximately at the market.

192. Thus far we have considered the protective function in relation to guaranty and marketability.

Marketability, you remember, is only one of the two sides of negotiability; only one of the forms of convertibility. Bonds do not have to be sold to be converted. They may be converted temporarily by hypothecation.

193. **The Bond Houses as Banks of Deposit.** We of the profession are inclined to take good humoredly, if not quite seriously, the efforts of the younger and therefore, perhaps, more ambitious bond houses to build up their business

THE BANKING FUNCTION 113

by the opening of interest-bearing deposit accounts—or whatever you would call them. The underlying motive is the same as that back of $100 pieces of bonds. Selfishly, to widen the clientele and educate to bond buying; unselfishly to encourage thrift in this very extravagant nation. Interest-bearing deposit accounts, subject to check, and bonds of $100 denomination are not in the same category as bonds bought on the instalment plan. Instalment bond buying has some of the same strength and weakness as ordinary insurance. It encourages "saving" to be sure, but it commits one to engagements one may not be able to fulfill. It is not investment, except when it has "paid up" value. But a deposit account with a bond house leaves you a free agent as to further transactions.

194. The other aspects of the banking function are not of sufficient importance to retail here, and they have little or no relation to the protective functions, about which we do well to center our attention.

195. **The Protective Function Applied to All Bond Qualities.** Up to this point the present paper has not dealt with that phase of the business which comes most quickly to mind when one speaks of the protective function. Broadly considered the protective function can be exercised—should be exercised—in the in-

114 THE PROTECTIVE FUNCTION

terest of any of the ten elements or good qualities that go to the making of an ideal investment. Those qualities, you will remember, were distinguished as follows:

Security of principal
Security (or stability) of income
Fair income return
Marketability ⎫
Value as collateral ⎬ Convertibility
Tax-exemption
Freedom from care
Acceptable duration
Acceptable denomination
Potential appreciation.

196. The action and interaction of these qualities, one upon another, and the part of the bond house in assisting the work, has just been fully illustrated. We have deliberated over the quality called marketability, and over the quality called hypothecary value (or value as collateral) and perhaps have convinced ourselves that in furthering these virtues in any investment a house is furthering the security of that investment.

197. So, also, the protective function may be extended over the whole elements or qualities, over some in greater degree than over others. As to the second of these, for instance: Stability of income—banking houses frequently pay the interest of railroad obliga-

THE BANKING FUNCTION 115

tions during a season of duress until reorganization plans perfect the ultimate adjustment of the loan. There may, of course, be an ulterior motive to the payment, such as to gain control of the issue in question, but again control is probably desired for concerted action for the benefit of the security holders. Bond houses are generally back of bondholders' protective committees. In the present difficulties of the Wabash there are operative just such measures protective of the coupons of the First Refunding and Extension 4s.

198. **Protecting Security.** But when all is said and done the protective function is most important in relation to the security of the invested principal. An ounce of prevention should have been applied in purchasing the issue to offer to clients. In want of the ounce, a pound of cure may be available. There are certain bond houses that for a few years past have yielded little or no return to their proprietors. The profits from merchandising have been devoted to the payment of losses for which these houses are not legally responsible, but which they voluntarily assume in the interest of their clients.

199. **Assuming Losses.** A member of one of the better New York houses illustrates the point as follows: "A group of bankers

handled the bonds of a hydro-electric company. The company had been in operation but a comparatively short time when a terrific flood carried away the dam and did other damage which virtually destroyed the power plant. The bankers came forward and reconstructed the dam and the power houses at a cost of about three-quarters of a million dollars. For their advances to the company they took junior securities, which have a very questionable value. It will be a great many years before the bankers will get back the money they advanced, if, in fact, they ever do. They took this action with a view only of protecting the interests of their clients, who had purchased the first mortgage bonds of the company. Had they not provided the funds for the reconstruction of the dam and plant their bondholders would have suffered heavy losses. The bankers, although they were not legally liable, preferred to make a heavy sacrifice rather than have their bondholders suffer."

200. **Protection in Reorganization.** The Street was agog last winter over an extraordinary Christmas gift voted the president of one of the big trust companies. This gift was the tribute of the board of directors to a talent for protecting distressed security holders and rehabilitating depleted properties. Reconstruction is almost as important as con-

THE BANKING FUNCTION 117

struction. Few of our great railroads have attained an investment level for their securities until they have been through one or two receiverships. The record of street railways is no better. As a class public utility companies have fared better than railroads because they came later and were developd (i. e., refinanced) by investment houses, not by speculative cliques; by institutions that had either a conscience or a sense that honesty is the best policy, not by buccaneers of finance who are in business for what they can get out of it—nothing more.

201. As I read the proof of this text before it goes to press a letter comes to me from a Connecticut investor containing the following:

"I could tell you of one dealer in securities who in the course of a dozen years or so has built up his business from practically nothing to a turnover of two or three millions a year, partly because he ascertained values, partly because he never misrepresented, and partly because he did his best to stand between his clients and loss. There are better ways of getting money out of people than by fleecing them and better ways of getting the value out of life."

202. The old and the new modes of American finance are very properly signalized by

the black death's head on the red field and the red cross on the white field, respectively. The supremacy of the latter emblem we owe to the highly developed protective function of the bond houses, and to the caution, among them, that the protective policy fosters.

CHAPTER VIII.

SELLING BONDS—THE BANKER'S VIEWPOINT.

203. However much we may emphasize the importance of various other bond house functions, it must be confessed that they are tributary to and exist by grace of the selling function. Bond firms are merchants of securities; they are in business to make money, not by trading in interest but by selling paper.

The Development of Bond Selling. If successful selling is the goal, then we should expect in the selling end of the business an expenditure of energy and attention, money and men, a concentration of vital force, out of all proportion to the other activities of the firm; and we find it. We should also expect well-established, generally accepted selling principles, that, when conscientiously followed, would lead to reasonably assured profits; but we don't find them.

204. There can be no question, now, that there is a science of bond investment, viz., of bond buying. The principles of bond investment, or bond buying, are the corpus of a new science: a branch of applied economics in the family tree of the sciences. There is *not yet*

a science of bond selling, in spite of the immense importance, and need, and money profit when that is developed.

205. It will not do to waive the matter aside by saying that salesmanship is an art. To be sure it is. So is conduct. But because conduct is an art there is no reason for overlooking the study of ethics, which is the branch of philosophy that forms the scientific basis for conduct. The verve, the force, the fire of successful salesmanship are not hindered but helped by cool calculation of the sources and efforts of enthusiasm, of the cost of competitive representation and of the most effective methods of publicity. What better proof can you have that salesmanship has *principles,* ergo, is a science, than the fact that good salesmanship is perpetuated in certain well-known industrial organizations after the brains that built the selling departments were transferred to other fields of activity? The cash register and automobile industries illustrate the point I am making.

206. **The Trouble with Bond Selling.** What then, it will be asked, is the trouble with bond selling? In what specific features does it fall short of reasonable efficacy? I believe thoughtful bond men will agree with me as to the weakness of the present system, although there may be no agreement regarding remedies.

THE BANKER'S VIEWPOINT 121

207. **The Cost of Selling.** The greatest weakness is the cost of selling securities,—the cost of distribution. The enlargement of organization and concentration of capital that are the chief characteristics of modern industry are permitted to exist, in spite of the evils engendered, because of the resulting lessened costs of producing and distributing commodities. It has been estimated—with what correctness I do not know—that the actual cost of producing and distributing the common articles of consumption has been lessened by about 2½ per cent. a year for the last few years. Parenthetically, if this be the case so much more glaring are the counteracting forces: an absurd tariff, congestion of population, a plethora of gold, and national extravagances,—that are steadily forcing upward prices the consumer has to pay. It is improbable that the cost of selling securities is lessening, for the number of small competitive houses is rapidly increasing and there is yet no tendency toward amalgamation.

208. **The Profit in Specialty Selling.** In speaking of the gross profit of from 5 to 15 points plus stock bonus made by the bond houses in their specialties, I contended that the amount was not excessive, considering the cost of distribution. I suppose in this case the cost of manufacture or production may be

considered to be the salaries and expenses of the buying and statistical force and a portion of the overhead charge. The cost of manufacture, so to speak, is small, relative to the selling cost, and therefore, negligible in this study.

209. However, a gross profit of 5 to 15 per cent. (more commonly 5 than 15) would be excessive under a modern, enlightened selling plan. No words then should be needed to convince the investing public that they have as vital an interest in the vending methods of the bond houses as they have in the way coal, oil, meat and milk are obtained and brought to their doors.

210. Probably most of those who read this article have some notion of the way bonds are sold—particularly high-yield bonds of little vogue or market, destined largely for the private investor. Each new issue means the circularization of almost the entire list of the issuing house, extensive advertising, the submission of offers by travelling salesmen who put up at the best hotels and cover an extensive territory, and the confirmation of these offers by correspondence. The number of circulars sent, miles travelled and days consumed by representatives, and letters written per $1,000 bond sold of profitable paper, would, however, probably open the eyes of the most

THE BANKER'S VIEWPOINT 123

sophisticated investor. So much for present costs.

211. I state with confidence born of observation that very, very few selling departments have at present, or have outlined for ultimate development, a selling program that intelligently seeks relief from excessive costs or in other ways evidences the result of constructive thinking. It is a hit or miss, catch-as-catch can game, won by those with the shrewdest instincts or backed by the most ample and patient capital. Future conditions in their entirety are unforeseeable to be sure, and the best laid plans go awry; you can't anchor even a time-defying educational institution to the purposes of its founders; but no business in these transitional days has a mortgage on the prosperity of the future that is not giving thought to present selling costs and is not receptive to changes in its sales policy, however radical, if they assure abatement of expenses with consequent betterment of strategic position with respect to other houses.

212. **Failures from Competition and Miscarriage of Issues.** The number of bond organizations is growing so rapidly, and the competition is becoming so keen, that the next ten years will probably see the downfall of a considerable number at least of the Eastern organizations, where the crowding is most no-

ticeable,—particularly of organizations that have succumbed to the temptation to take profitable turnovers rather than unquestionable paper. The intention may be of the best,—but then we all know of a place said to be paved with good intentions. If a few issues "go wrong on a house" some of the clients may be willing to forgive and forget, but human nature is human nature, and the recollection of mishaps outlives the memory of splendid successes.

213. Until the weeding out process is accomplished by miscarriage of bond issues or inability to make expenses over a series of lean investment years we may expect an aggravation of the state of things recently described to me by an Albany salesman. You know every salesman considers his territory is the worst in the world from a selling point of view. In Boston, to be sure, every third man buys bonds, but then, every second man sells them. In northern Pennsylvania there are fewer bond men but nobody buys bonds. So it goes. Well, to get back to Albany: I said, "Jones, how's the competition these days up at the capital?" "Competition!" he replied, grieved at the question. "There is none. We all walk up State street lock step and toss up to see who goes in to brace our man and find out there's nothing doing."

THE BANKER'S VIEWPOINT 125

214. Selling Economies: Consolidation of Houses. A first move to better security distribution is suggested quite naturally by the evolution of industry: a consolidation of bond houses. We have seen the consolidation of manufacturers, of middlemen, and of producers of raw material. Later the manufacturers absorbed the middlemen, and still later, many of the producers. It has taken strenuous Federal activity to keep the agencies of transportation out of the same encompassment. Most recently, and as rapidly as ever before in industry, there has been coagulation among the banks, particularly of course in New York. Why not then a union of bond houses, which are middlemen between the coalescing producers of securities and the coalescing financial institutions that consume securities?

215. There are very obvious advantages in any possible union of the agencies of security distribution, not the least of which is the greater range in choice of issues made possible by the augmented capital, resources, and distributing power. Moreover, duplicate representation in selling would cease. Equally important, perhaps, overhead economies are possible just as in non-financial industry.

216. There is no need to go into particulars; the advantages will be conceded. Why then is no tendency observable toward the con-

solidation of bond houses? Is it not for the same reason that Massachusetts "Tech" and Harvard did not consolidate a few years ago; for the same reason that physicians do not usually practise as firms? I admit neither analogy is perfect. Property considerations influenced the two Massachusetts universities, and physicians have relatively unimportant "over-heads" to curtail. But nevertheless, there is a point to be made. In a greater or less degree, according to the quality of each firm, the bond houses stand in that professional relation to their clients which I have emphasized, so that the selling value of their sponsorship of issues would be impaired by partial loss of identity and personality occasioned by consolidation. A firm is slow to relinquish, in the interest of economy, a professional relationship and standing that have taken years of the hardest kind of effort to achieve. The two strongest influences affecting bond sales are the character of the house and liking for the salesman. Amalgamation would mean serious impairment of at least half their claim upon clients.

217. **Local Representation.** There has been a development in bond selling that is away from direct competitive representation, namely the representation of one or more houses by a local dealer. Many New York houses have

THE BANKER'S VIEWPOINT 127

tried this experiment in territory that apparently could not support a travelling salesman. The result has been unsatisfactory. The local dealer is seldom trained to the profession. If trained the chances are he is not in special sympathy with the policies of the home office. He can hardly serve two or more masters. Even when he represents one house, if he is successful, his temptation is to cut loose as a free agent and make void all the pains taken to set him on his feet.

218. **Bank Representation.** Another form of local representation yields more promise of ultimate success. For some years past bond departments have been springing up rapidly in all kinds of banks and trust companies in all parts of the country. At first the movement was discredited as ephemeral, but the continued existence of many of the older departments and the multiplication of new departments indicates that they have a useful place in security distribution. The bond houses, therefore, must take them into consideration.

219. In the nature of things the majority of these bank bond departments must act as security brokers. They may venture with safety to buy local issues of municipals, and the old line railroad paper in which there is no profit; but they are not technically equipped to investigate, buy and sell entire issues of

corporation bonds. For the business that is most worth while they must look to the bond houses proper. Perhaps, therefore, in time, a group of bond houses can coalesce, territorially, if they cannot amalgamate corporately, and eliminate some of the waste in competitive representation, by selling through the banks.

220. This method of security distribution through local banks has foreign precedent and practice to recommend it. But it is not the solution of all our difficulties. Indirect representation relieves the issuing house of a large part of the selling cost, but also of a large part of its responsibility. This is not a theory but a fact, evidenced here and abroad, now and in the past. The issuing house has less sense of responsibility regarding the character of its loans and regarding the market for them prior to maturity. Indirect representation also relieves the issuing house of a part of its profits, thus defeating in part at least the object it seeks.

221. I must confess, when all is said and done, that the first relief from present conditions will probably not come from any deliberate change in selling policy, but from the slower and more certain working of economic law. The fittest will survive the coming decade of debt-readjustment: those who have sold bonds that do not go wrong.

THE BANKER'S VIEWPOINT

222. The Economy of Selling Collateral Trusts. At this point I wish to venture a suggestion, for whatever it may be worth, that may ultimately have a decided bearing on the development of bond selling. Of recent years certain houses have had a conspicuous success in distributing collateral trust bonds, secured by miscellaneous issues that are the first mortgage obligations of companies doing one kind of business. One house specializes in what might be called collateral trust water bonds, several, in collateral trust lighting bonds (gas and electric), several in collateral trust real estate bonds, etc.

223. The principle of safety in these collateral trust issues lies in a distributed risk plus technical excellence in a particular industrial field through specialization on the part of the issuing company. The income, from which the interest is paid, may be derived in two general ways: (a) through stock dividends to the parent company by ownership of the subsidiary companies which have pledged their bonds, or (b) through bond interest, by payment of the interest of the pledged bonds to the trustee of the collateral trust, to be applied to the payment of interest of the collateral trust bonds. Obviously the second method is the sounder, for it gives a more direct and prior hold on the income of the subsidiaries.

224. The principle of marketability has not, I believe, been given the attention it deserves, in these bonds, largely because the collateral trust houses (if I may so speak of them), are not usually and primarily banking houses, but the security-selling departments of engineering houses, mortgage dealers, or what not.

225. Marketability usually implies quality in the bond, demand for it, and a clearing house or security exchange for the convenient, recognized place of purchase and sale of it. I am a hearty believer in the possibilities for safety in a *properly drawn* collateral trust agreement, when the collateral widely distributes the risk: granting safety, the demand for the collateral trust bond will be largely determined by the size of the issue. Other things being equal the larger the issue the greater its vogue. This fact I emphasized in the chapter on Buying Railroad Bonds. One of the chief causes for the refunding of divisional railroad mortgages by big blanket liens is the enhancement of investment value by the increased marketability of the large general and refunding loan.

226. If, now, true banking bond houses will enter the field as sponsors for good open-end collateral trust issues of sufficient quality and ultimate size to develop a constantly growing investment demand, and will act openly

THE BANKER'S VIEWPOINT 131

as the clearing house for transactions in the issues, at least until they become listed on the New York Stock Exchange, these houses may find, as each new instalment of the loan is floated, that the selling cost has been materially reduced without proportionate reduction in profits.

227. **Consolidation of Issues not Houses.** Indeed I should not be at all surprised if the ultimate solution of the present cost of security distribution was not consolidation of *houses,* but of *issues* under the collateral trust form. And I am the more confident that this is a sound position to take as I consider the lessened cost of railroad security selling in this country and of real estate security selling in Western Europe, with increase of safety for the investments.

228. This suggested broader application of the collateral trust is not iconoclasm. Indeed if it were, what of it? Severe ills require heroic remedies. Whatever *is* is not necessarily best in finance; witness our currency system. One does not wish to appear a prophet of evil; but unless all signs fail there will be drastic readjustment of security issuance and security selling long before the mass of long term paper we are now disposing of is presented for redemption. The tide of a ten-year prosperity has turned against us

and it is high time the live fish start to swim up against the stream.

229. **The Selling Department of an Ideal Bond House.** However, taking things as we find them, a word as to the selling department of an ideal bond house. An ideal bond house, by the way, is a financial Chateau en Espagne that does its best work on paper. Some of the unusual regulations of this house, I myself have tried with a share of success; all of them have been tried by somebody; but the organization, as such, will be the first of its kind all under one roof.

230. **The Sales Manager.** In the first place you must have a sales manager, who must manage,—on whom all responsibility must fall, and also a fair share of the profits and losses. We have not yet got beyond the one-man power in the bond business, any more than in any other business. Every man in the selling end should be of his choosing from the office boys to the territorial managers, or overseers, for the office boys might just as well be fellows just out of college who want to go on the road later, and the territorial managers (of whom there ought to be one to every six road men) are responsible for the money made or lost in their territory. The sales manager will have a spirit and business policy that in time will stamp his entire business family.

THE BANKER'S VIEWPOINT 133

231. **Territorial Managers.** Your territorial managers are men who have been advanced from the road,—not necessarily because they are the best salesmen, but because they are built to get results out of others. They have been advanced for the most part from your own force, not imported from other houses to intrude an alien spirit and plan into an otherwise cohesive organization. They know the name and holdings and predilections of all the clients in their particular territory. They know who is in funds and when; they remind their men, and see that the proper kind and amount of correspondence is circulating among these clients. They go over each man's route with him once a year at least and meet all his business friends who appear worth while. They correspond daily with each of their salesmen, keeping him informed of all financial happenings, inspiriting him, making suggestions, and in general increasing his efficiency. On his return to the office every two weeks, they review the progress made, outline the salient features of new issues to be sold and in general revitalize spirits that for the first few years are likely to sag when business isn't good.

232. The sales manager and his territorial assistants will be a court of last resort to which all "specialties" that have met the ap-

proval of the buying department will be submitted for acceptance. The issue in some instances may be carried a step further and be submitted to a few or all of the salesmen for discussion. The more responsibility you place on a good man the more you can expect of and get out of him. It is also well to stop in advance the mouth of the man who is always going to do something big, but never has the right bond.

233. **The Road Men.** Now as to the road men themselves,—a large number, perhaps most, will be college men for several reasons. The calling will bring them into contact with the very best classes of people, men in positions of trust, and men and women who have sufficient talent to accumulate funds or who have had the benefits of inherited means. College men as a class are more acceptable and congenial to such people than relatively *inexperienced* men who are not college bred. Any bond house can get all the college men it wants *if it goes after them,* at very small expense, because they are not experienced. What you want is the right raw material. All men not bred to your policies are raw material. Men not college bred, *of the same age,* are failures already if they would accept the $5 or $10 a week a green man in the bond business is given by good houses.

THE BANKER'S VIEWPOINT 135

234. As for myself I believe in seeking what you are after along any line. For some years I have visited one or more colleges and annually have laid the advantages and disadvantages of the bond business as a career before 25 to 100 seniors and graduates, discouraging 95 per cent. at sight and cautioning the other 5 per cent. not to come unless they would rather sell than eat. Life is too short.

235. **College Men as Salesmen.** College men have one distinct disadvantage. Education induces reflection, and reflection often saps the dynamic spontaneity that is a salesman's best asset. However, any house (there are such) that is striving to elevate its services for the community to the plane of the professions, will recruit its forces largely out of the college class, from which professional men are recruited, trusting by superior organization and esprit du corps to supply what may be lacking in Yankee vending instinct. There are salesmen and salesmen. One can sell collar buttons, another horses, and still another bonds.

236. **The Training of Green Men.** Turn loose half-a-dozen to a dozen of these green men in your main office. Let them run errands and make deliveries so that they will imagine themselves useful. Have them at once begin reading the financial dailies and asking ever-

lasting questions. In a few weeks, when their heads have stopped swimming, start a class and teach them the difference between finance and the grocery business, between bonds and stocks, between municipals and industrials. Later have them study the house's issues and the more important issues of other houses as they appear from time to time. Later still have them read some of the incoming and outgoing mail that they may get some idea of the investor's point of view, the salesman's problems, and the gentle art of persuading people to exchange what they have for what you have. Above all (and generally most neglected), develop a sense of current quotations and intrinsic values.

237. If a salesmanager is a judge of character and picks his men with discretion and *systematically* trains them, in a year's time he should turn out on the road a crew of which one in three should make good. Any house that can develop one loyal, successful salesman out of every three recruits can make money if it buys the right kind of bonds to sell.

CHAPTER IX.

SELLING BONDS—THE INVESTOR'S VIEWPOINT.

238. **The Strength of the Investment Demand.** It may be worth while, when considering the investor's interest in bond selling principles and methods, first to take stock of the investor himself, to gauge as accurately as may be the volume and strength of his investment requirements. No direct statistical means are available for a correct estimate. Only by collateral measurements can we justly apprehend the demand.

239. There is food for reflection in the argument of the United States Steel Corporation against the move for dissolution that its owners number over 100,000. The very great majority of these owners are American citizens who have bought to invest, not to speculate.

240. **Savings Banks as Bond Buyers.** The number of savings bank depositors in the United States is nearly 10,000,000, or 12 per cent. of the population, men, women and children. The aggregate deposits are about $4,250,000,000.

The spirit of saving, therefore of investment, is rapidly growing. One year's increase in

138 SELLING BONDS—

savings bank depositors is 650,000; of deposits, $142,000,000; the increase per depositor is $13.

The indirect interest that American savings bank depositors have in bond selling is this: Of the $4,250,000,000 they have intrusted to saving institutions to invest for them, about $1,850,000,000, or 43 per cent., has been used to buy bonds.

241. The Volume of Municipal Bond Sales. Our powers of security absorption may be apprehended somewhat when we observe that during the past year there were recorded original government and municipal bond sales in the United States aggregating $636,000,000 and comprising 4,891 different issues. One may say truly that only a very small part of these issues will ever leave the country.

242. Annual Listings on the Exchange. During the same year the new note issues of record that reached the New York market amounted to $310,000,000; and the new bond listings on the New York Stock Exchange to $580,000,000, of which $298,000,000 were railroad, $34,000,000 street railway, and $248,000,000 miscellaneous loans. The exchange listings exceeded $1,000,000,000 in one year (1909).

243. The Obscure Issues. There is very little duplication in these figures for 1911. Very few millions of the civil loans or notes were listed. In addition to this vast debt there were the few municipal and the countless private corporation loans that did not or could not become matters of public record. But whatever the true amount of funded debt emitted that year the great bulk of it was sold, or will ultimately be sold, to investors, in blocks large and small, and in single bonds, by the American bond houses.

244. If now we appreciate the genuine interest and importance of sound bond buying by the American people, whether this interest is direct or indirect, we are prepared to consider some suggestions regarding sound bond selling by the bond houses to the American people. These I shall take up in their natural sequence.

245. **The Investor Should Know his Own Requirements.** In the first place, however conscientious your bankers may be, they seldom appreciate to the full what are your own particular investment needs. If the business pace were not so fast, if the selling instinct were not so strongly developed at the expense of the advisory, the case might be different. There is no reason, in the nature of things, why a banker should not know what you want better than you yourself, just as your physician knows better than you what regimen is most suited for your physical welfare. But we have to accept the facts as we find them.

246. Complex Nature of Security. It is not sufficient, for perfect service, that you want a good bond which you can sell again, or even that you want an absolutely safe bond which is readily marketable. Safety and marketability in an investment are like goodness in anything—purely relative terms. The Pennsylvania Convertible Debenture 3½s of 1915 are safe and marketable, so are the Norfolk and Western First Consolidated 4s of 1996 (to pick issues at random), but there is a wide range of degrees in safety and marketability between these two good bonds.

247. Safety itself is not a simple thing, but (again like goodness) it is a very complex quality. It is for you to realize what kind of safety you most require. I have frequently emphasized the various qualities of investment safety or security, labelling two to emphasize the fact of differences: *security in redemption,* and *security in liquidation.* A high degree of security in redemption means an approximate certainty that at maturity the principal of your investment will be paid. A high degree of security in liquidation means an approximate certainty that at any time you may sell your investment at small loss, if any.

248. When the chances are slight that you will want to sell before maturity then you are more concerned with security in redemption.

When you are investing the deposits of a national bank and may be forced at any time to realize to meet the demands of depositors, you may be equally concerned with security in liquidation.

249. The bonds of the United States illustrate well the various qualities of security. As models of safety they are held up to the point of weariness. They will be paid. Oh, yes. Even in panics their fluctuation now is slight, averaging not much over four points. What more could be asked? Well, to be quite perfect, to convince us that security is an absolute, not a relative, term, we should have to forget that in Civil War times they sold on a basis to yield from 6 to 12 per cent.; that in the process of currency reform, it is possible, though perhaps not probable, that their withdrawal as the basis of circulation would do to their quotations what a panic does to railroad bond quotations. Possible, though not probable, because the purpose of the Government seems expressed in the Aldrich measure, which provides for a gradual conversion of the Federal loans that secure note issues. But possibility as well as probability are factors of the unknown and undependable—factors of insecurity. Therefore, even the security for "governments" is adapted to analysis and discrimination.

250. Complex Nature of Marketability. Marketability is equally susceptible to study. Here is an issue of listed railroad refunding bonds. At present $13,000,000 are outstanding. If well distributed but not permanently locked in the strong boxes of savings banks and insurance companies, they may be turned over at the average rate of $120,000 a month, let us say. But the authorization is $175,000,000, and next year they retire and take the place of an underlying issue of $35,000,000. Whatever detriment this impending flotation may be to your security in liquidation, the marketability is certainly bound to improve unless the issue deteriorates through impairment of the obligor's earning power.

251. Now for another aspect. If you may be called upon to dispose, within a day or a week, of a block of $100,000 bonds, you need an entirely different kind of market for your issue than if you have $5,000 bonds that never would have to be sold on less than three months' notice. It is very much easier to sell without sacrifice $100,000 Pennsylvania Convertible 3½s in a hurry than $100,000 Norfolk and Western First Consolidated 4s; but if you own only one Norfolk and Western you do not have this to consider. It is usually easier to sell coupon than registered bonds, railroad than municipal bonds, municipal than corporation bonds.

THE INVESTOR'S VIEWPOINT 148

252. You are concerned in knowing exactly the kind and amount of safety and marketability you require because you have to pay for them. You do not demand *more* safety and marketability than you require because then you are dissipating a part of your investment in paying for what you don't need; perhaps you are sacrificing some security of principal for superfluous marketability. To pay $1,100 for an investment that gives you only $1,050 worth of investment service is not conservatism but extravagance. Nothing but unfamiliarity with investment principles is an excuse for private buying of United States bonds to net 2½ per cent. The Federal Government encourages this merely to prevent the worse habit of hoarding. It does not seek or want for its 2½ per cent. funds the money of *investors*.

253. Of the ten principal investment qualities that I have mentioned repeatedly in these articles, safety and marketability have been chosen for amplification here, as those most in the public mind. What has been said of them applies, if with somewhat less force, to security of income, hypothecary value, convenience of duration and denomination, freedom from taxation and care, possibility of appreciation, and whatever other qualities you may care to consider.

254. Second Consideration: Form of the Investment. Having taken this first and most important step of considering your investment needs, it is next in order for you to consider what *form* of investment is best to satisfy these needs, mindful that investment, with the advantages and disadvantages peculiar to it, is a thing apart from speculation. If investment is the proper channel for your surplus, and if you canvass your situation most thoroughly, you will probably find that bonds, which have just served us for illustration of the scope of investment qualities, are probably the best form of investment for you. At least it may be said in truth that the infinite varieties of bonds cover more requirements than any other investment form.

255. Third Consideration: Proper Type of Bond. The third step is to find the type or types of bonds that are best adapted to your definitely predetermined needs; the fourth, to find the best issue of the type selected.

256. Here is the only thoroughly sound procedure for the selection and purchase of securities, yet how few advocate it, or pursue it! Some banks and insurance companies that buy largely and constantly have a well developed and consistent buying policy, as bond men know, but they are exceptions to custom.

257. Many investors have definite rules

THE INVESTOR'S VIEWPOINT 145

governing their purchases, but such rules! One of my good friends to whom I used to sell will buy any Massachusetts municipals, but will not go over the line into New York or Connecticut. It is not taxation that troubles him, either. Just an amiable insularity. Another friend will buy municipals anywhere, but nothing else. A commission house that buys many thousands a year looks for the best issue that at the time yields 5 per cent. In the panic it was Eastern municipals from banks that had to disgorge. Now it may be mortgage liens on the minor railroads. Some will buy no paper from the South; many will buy only first mortgages. This is all wrong. As Dr. Johnson would say, such rules are merely evidences of temperamental anfractuosities.

258. As we stop to think of it, there is something, though not much, to be said for the man who narrowly and arbitrarily limits the range of his investments. He can, and probably does, become more familiar with the channel he has chosen for his funds, and so is able to avoid the seduction of "unusual opportunities." At the same time he limits the chance to distribute his risk. This limit is the more serious if his chosen channel is in itself unsafe. The range of quality in bond types is almost as great as the range of quality in issues of any type.

259. One of the most striking illustrations of ill-considered bond-buying is the quick disposal by subscription sale of immense corporation issues before the indentures securing the issues are made public. Truly we do business on faith these days. To be sure, confidence of this sort is not often misplaced, but how would you like to put a considerable part of your personal fortune into a bond, only to find, when the deed of trust finally appeared in print, that, the Court permitting, the owner of a majority of the outstanding bonds could compel acquiescence from the minority to *any* change in the terms of the deed of trust?

260. The indenture of one of the bond issues that has been most prominently before the public this past year reads as follows:

"From time to time the holders of a majority in amount of all the . . . bonds hereby secured for the time being outstanding, by their vote at a meeting of the holders of said . . . bonds, . . . or by an instrument or instruments in writing signed by such holders, shall have the power (1) to assent to and authorize any modification or compromise of the rights of the holders of such class of bonds and of the Trustee for the holders of such class of bonds, against the . . . Company or against any property subject to this indenture, whether such rights shall arise under these presents or

THE INVESTOR'S VIEWPOINT 147

otherwise, and (2) to assent to and authorize any modification of any of the provisions of this indenture that shall be proposed by the . . . Company and recommended by the Trustee. . . . Any action taken with the assent or authority given as aforesaid of the holders of a majority in amount of the . . . bonds hereby secured, for the time being outstanding, shall be binding upon the holders of all the . . . bonds hereby secured and upon the Trustee as fully as though such action was specifically and expressly authorized by the terms of this indenture."

261. It is customary, of course, for trust deeds to contain waivers of certain specific rights of the bondholders upon vote of a substantial majority, but observe in this clause what might happen if the obligor should purchase or otherwise control 51 per cent. of the issue. Of course the moral is: Never buy a bond without reading the mortgage and trust deed.

Recent discussion of this issue, in and out of the courts and the press, would fill volumes; yet nowhere have I seen comment on these significant lines quoted above, which he who runs may read.

262. **Fourth Consideration: The Proper Bond.** The "average investor" may well feel that, even if he has a definite idea of the

qualities he needs in his bond, and even if he reads with assiduity the mortgages and financial statements of various current issues, he is still unprepared to do himself justice. He is right. He cannot be expected to know his own business, if he has any, and the bond business also. Hence the need of establishing clientelary relations with a bond house that has a sense of professional responsibility, and the equipment for superior service.

263. **Choosing a Bond House.** To find, then, the best bond for his needs, the investor will obtain the assistance of a good house that handles as part of its regular business the type of bond in question. If he does not know of any such house, he will do well to consult the local bank presidents and directors, who can obtain the information from unprejudiced sources if they do not have it at hand. A number of inquiries should be made to average away incorrect information. Other things being equal, it is better to align oneself with a house or houses that have local or transient representatives, for oral discussion, always supplemented by home-office correspondence, is much more satisfactory than the correspondence alone.

264. With thorough knowledge of his own requirements and a proper banking relation established the investor can hardly go astray.

He has quite reversed the customary procedure, for instead of choosing a random bond from a random house and trusting that it will serve his purpose, he has first inquired of himself what his purpose is and he has set in motion in his behalf the highly intelligent machinery of one of the best and most honorably conducted kinds of business organization. If anything, he will be rather skeptical about a new loan (unless it be municipal) and encourage his advisers to submit a considerable number of seasoned issues of the proper type.

265. In closing these comments, let me express the hope that they will leave an impression on readers that may be summed up in a remark made to me by the manager of a great Canadian banking house, when I joined the bond fraternity: "Chamberlain, this business, like every other, has its disadvantages, but one thing you may be sure of, you will never have to make apologies for your profession."

INDEX

Advertisement by bond houses of the marketability of their bonds, 32.
Advertising, bond, 166-171; of investment principles, 169.
Advising a woman, 152.
Advisory advertisement, 169, 171.
Advisory function, 20-22, Chap. VI, 152 et seq.
Amount of municipal bond sales in the United States, 241.
Analyzing a municipal statement, difficulty of, 87.
Annual bond listings on the Exchange, 242.
Artificial marketability, cost of, to investors, 185; to the bond houses, 190, 191.
Assuming losses, 199.
Attorneys for municipal bond houses, competency of, 72.
Auditor, the, in bond buying, 139.

Bank representation, local, in bond selling, 218.
Bankers vs. Brokers, 4.
Banking function, 23; Chap. VII, 174 et seq; 189 et seq.
Bankruptcy, see Default, Receivership, Reorganization, etc.
Banks, local, as bond distributors, 31.
Banks of deposit, the bond houses as, 193.
Bidding for bonds, see Buying, Municipal Bonds, etc.
Blanket railroad refunding issues, 104 et seq; amount outstanding, 106.
Bond advertising, 166-171; attorneys, municipal, competency of, 72; dealers vs. brokers, 4.
Bond business, ignorance of, 2; importance of, 1.
Bond guaranty, 176-181.
Bond houses as banks of deposit, 193; as constructors, 150; as fiscal agents, 24, 25; as reorganizers, 149; as specialists, 134.
Bond houses, consolidation of, 26; functions of, Chap. I and esp. 5; influence of, on municipal finance, 19; American enterprise, 9.
Bond houses vs. brokers, stability of, 8; wholesale vs. retail, 6, 7.
Bond investment as a science, 35 et seq.

INDEX

Bond sales, municipal in the United States, 241.
Bonds, American, who buys them, 1; total annual issuance in America, 1; as collateral, 187-189.
Brokers vs. Bankers, 4.
Bureaus of financial information, 42-44; 165; of municipal bond information, 80.
Business conditions, forecasting, 45, 46.
Buying bonds in New England, 3; bonds to satisfy clients, 48; corporation bonds, 12 et seq; municipal bonds, 10 et seq; railroad bonds, Chap. IX, 88 et seq.

Capitalization as affecting railroad bond security, 119.
Carrying charges in relation to bond selling profits, 75.
Census reports as a statistical help, 43.
Choosing a bond house, 34; 263.
Circulars of bond issues, special, 171.
Classification of bonds, 123 et seq.
Collateral, bonds as, 187-189; collateral trust issues, economy of selling, 222 et seq.
College men as bond salesmen, 29; 235-237.
Common characteristics of railroad and municipal bonds, 89.
Community of interest as affecting railroad bond security, 115.
Competition among industries forcing amalgamation, 148, 149; in bond selling, 26 et seq; 212, 213.
Complex nature of marketability, 250; of security, 246 et seq.
Consolidation of bond houses, 26, 30 et seq; of bond issues, 214 et seq.
Construction propositions, 18; bond house financing of, 150.
Corporation bond investment principles, 126.
Corporation bonds, newness of, 135; buying, 12 et seq.
Correspondence, investment by, 172, 173.
Cost of artificial marketability, to investors, 185; to the bond houses, 190, 191; bond guaranty, 178, 179; of bond selling, 207 et seq; of distribution of bonds, 145; of marketability, 32, 33; of selling bonds, 73; of supporting the market for municipal, railroad and specialty bonds, 89.

Dartmouth College, Tuck School of Finance, studying the effect of business conditions on corporation earnings, 132.

INDEX

Dealers vs. brokers, 4.
Declination of municipal issues on the score of legality, etc., 71.
Default (see receivership, reorganization, etc.), attitude of bond houses toward, 33.
Depositors in United States Savings Banks, number of, 240.
Depositors in United States Savings Banks, amount of, 240.
Development of bond selling, 203 et seq.
Directorate, bond house representation on, 16; 25.
Distribution of bonds, cost of, 145.
Domination of large corporations by wholesale houses, 92 et seq.

Earning power as affecting railroad bond security, 119.
Earnings in relation to fixed charges and safety, 15.
Economy of selling collateral trust issues, 222 et seq.
Effect of interest rates on bond buying, 54, 55.
Elements of an ideal investment, 59, 60; 253; three most prominent, 62.
Engineer, the, in bond buying, 139.
English selling methods, 163.
Equipment bonds, 109, 110.
Ethics of salesmanship, 154-163.

Failures of bond houses from competition and miscarriage of issues, 212.
Financial agents, see fiscal agents.
Financial news and report agencies, 42-44; 165; for municipal buying, 80.
Financial jackals, 156-160.
Fiscal agents, bond houses, as, 24, 25.
Forecasting business conditions, 45, 46.
Form of investment, must be considered by buyers, 254.
French and German banks as advisers, 21.
Function of the bond houses, the principal, 64.
Functions of the bond houses, Chap. I and esp. 5.
Fundamental conditions, forecasting, 45, 46.

Gas companies, 129.
General market bonds vs. "legals," 69 et seq.
General market municipals, 81.
General publicity as a form of bond house advertisement, 168.

INDEX 153

German and French banks as advisers, 21.
Government bonds, 249; reports as statistical help, 43.
Gravel road bonds of Indiana, legality of, 85.
Guaranty, bond, 176-181.

History of bond dealers, 4.
Hypothecation of bonds in relation to bond selling profits, 75.

Ideal bond house, selling department of, 229 et seq.
Illegitimate bond dealer, an, 51.
Importance of the bond business, 1.
Income of public service corporations, a study of, 132.
Indiana gravel road bonds, legality of, 85.
Industrial issues, easy for bankers to get good, 137.
Industrial corporation bonds, 13.
Insurance principle in bond guaranty, 177.
Influence of bondhouses on management of corporations, 25.
Interest rates, effect of rise in, on bond buying, 54, 55; affected by general interest rates, 55.
Invalidity of municipal bonds, amount of, 71.
Investor should know his own requirements, 245.
Investment, bond dealers vs. brokers, 4; correspondence, 172, 173; in the United States, strength of, 238 et seq; elements, the ten, 59, 60; 253; the three most prominent, 62; in bonds of United States Savings Banks, 240.
Irrigation bonds, 13.
Issues of bonds, total each year in America, 1.

Knowing the business of the corporation, 127 et seq.

Laboratory methods in bond buying, 37 et seq.
Legality of issuance and legality for savings bank investment, 71.
"Legals" vs. general market bonds, 69 et seq.
Libraries of bond houses, 37, etc.
Listings of bonds on the Exchange, annual amount, 242.
Local bank buying of municipals, 77.
Local bond representation, 217.
Losses, assumption of, by bond houses, 199.

Magnitude in relation to safety, 6, 7.
Management and proprietorship as affecting railroad bond security, 112-117.

INDEX

Management in relation to bond safety, 16; of corporations, influence of bond houses on, 25.

Managers, of the bond house, 230 et seq.

Marketability, artificial, cost of, to investors, 185; to the bond houses, 190, 191; as affected by the protective function, 182-188; as part of the protective function, 32 et seq; complex nature of, 250; cost of, 32, 33; in relation to big refunding issues, 105; of collateral trusts, 225 et seq; specialty vs. listed bonds, 32, 33.

Massachusetts legals and bond house responsibility, 71.

Massachusetts taxation in relation to bond dealers, 52, 53.

Mercantile vs. the protective policy, 174.

Mining bonds, 13.

Moody's Magazine calls attention to the rise in interest rates, 54.

Mortgages, reading, before bond buying, 95.

Municipal bond attorneys, competency of, 72; bond bureaus, 80.

Municipal bonds, buying, 10 et seq; declined on score of legality, etc., 71.

Municipal bond sales in the United States, amount of, 241.

Municipal default and repudiation, 83.

Municipal sale, an unintelligent, 79.

Municipal sales record as an aid to bidding, 76.

Municipalities selling bonds over the counter, 74.

New England, prevalence of bond buying in, 3.

New York legals and bond house responsibility, 71.

New York Stock Exchange, annual listings of bonds on, 242; bonds first offered and sponsored by bond houses, 1.

Newness of corporation bonds, 135.

Norfolk and Western First Consolidated 4s, 251.

Obscure issues of bonds, the, 243.

Oklahoma's experience with bank deposit guarantees, 181.

One man buying, 40, 41.

Output of American bonds each year, 1.

"Over-the-counter" selling of bonds by municipalities, 74.

Overcapitalization, 14.

INDEX 155

Pennsylvania Convertible 3½s, 251.
Pennsylvania Railroad flotation, a, 101.
Per capita debt of water companies, 128.
Physical characteristics of railroads as affecting railroad bond security, 118.
Physical condition, examination of, 17.
Preference for public utilities, 140.
Press as an influence in bond selling, 166.
Prevalence of bond buying in New England, 3.
Principal function of the bond houses, 64.
Profession, the bond business as a, 22; 28; 30; 35 et seq; 155; 162.
Professional Standard of bond houses, 49-53.
Profit in selling bonds in general, 141; in selling blanket refunding issues, 107; in selling corporation bonds, 142-145; legal municipals, 74; in selling railroad bonds, 89; in selling specialty bonds, 208, 209.
Profits in railroad bond underwriting and selling, 96 et seq.
Protecting security, 198; the market when local banks distribute, 31.
Protective function, 31 et seq; Chap. VII, 174; applied to all bond qualities, 195 et seq; applied to marketability, 182-188.
Proper bond, the, for each individual, 261.
Proper type of bond must be considered by buyers, 254.
Proprietorship and management as affecting railroad bond security, 112-117.
Public Utility bonds, banking competition for, 138.
Purchasing function, Chap. I, 10 et seq; Chap. II.

Quasi-municipals, the problem of buying, 69.

Railroad blanket refunding issues, 104 et seq; amount outstanding, 106.
Railroad bond investment principles, 111 et seq.
Railroad bond underwriting, 92 et seq.
Railroads as scientific financiers, 47.
Real Estate bonds commonly guaranteed, 180.
Records of past municipal sales as an aid to bidding, 76.
Receivership (see Default, Reorganization, etc.) attitude of bond houses toward, 33.
Refunding issues, railroad, 104 et seq; amount outstanding, 106.
Reorganization (see Receivership, Default, etc.) attitude of bond house toward, 33; importance of, 200.

INDEX

Reorganizers, the bond houses as, 149.
Repudiation of State debts between 1870 and 1884, 68; 81, 82.
Retail vs. wholesale bond houses, 6, 7.
Riddlebergers, the, 68.
Rise in interest rates, 54.
Road men, of the bond house, 233 et seq.

Sales Manager, in bond buying, 139; of the bond house, 230; 232; 237.
Sales of municipal bonds in the United States, 241.
Salesmanship, ethics of, 154-163.
Salesmen, bond, 29; of wholesale houses, 5.
Savings bank bonds, see "legals."
Savings bank bonds, small profit in selling, 50; United States, amount of deposits, number of depositors, investments of, 240.
Science, as applied to bond selling, a thing of the future, 204; bond investment as, 35 et seq; in railroad finance, 47.
Security, as affecting "legals," 71; complex nature of, 246 et seq.
Selling bonds, cost of, 73.
Selling department of an ideal bond house, 229 et seq.
Selling function, 26 et seq; Chap. VIII, 203 et seq; Chap. IX, 238 et seq.
Selling legal municipals, profit in, 74; of bonds by municipalities "over the counter," 74; profits in railroad bonds, 89.
"Services," financial news, etc., 42-44; 165; for municipal buying, 80.
Size, importance of in municipal bonds, 84.
Special census reports as statistical help, 43.
Special counsel in bond buying, 39.
"Special circulars" of bond issues, 171.
Specialists, bond houses as, 134.
Specialty selling, the profit in, 208, 209.
Spirit of trusteeship, 175 et seq.
Stability of bond houses vs. brokers, 8.
Standardization, in the bond business, 26; of business service, 136; of the railroad refunding issues, 106.
Statistical material as a help to bond buying, 130; 132, 133.
Statistician, the, in bond buying, 139.
Statistics and statistical departments, 36 et seq.
Statistics of municipal sales as an aid to bidding, 76.

INDEX 157

Stock bonuses, 56.
Stock Exchange, see New York Stock Exchange.
Street railways, printed information concerning, 131.
Strength of the investment demand in the United States, 238 et seq.
Subscription to bond underwriting (see Underwriting), 259 et seq.
Sub-underwriting, 93 et seq.

Taxation in Massachusetts in relation to bond dealers, 52, 53.
Telephone business, 127.
Ten investment elements, the, 59, 60; 253.
Tennessee Settlements, the, 68.
Territorial managers, the, of the bond house, 231, 232.
Three most prominent investment qualities, 62.
Traveling salesmen, 29; 233 et seq; of wholesale houses, 5.
Trouble with bond selling, 206.
Trusteeship, spirit of, 175 et seq.
Tuck School of Finance, Dartmouth College, studying the effect of business conditions on corporation earnings, 132.
Type of bond, proper, must be considered by buyers, 254.

Underwriting, 259 et seq; by retail houses, 93 et seq; railroad bonds, 92 et seq.
Unintelligent proposals for municipals, 79.
United States bonds, 249.
United States Steel Corporation, character of ownership, 239.

Volume of municipal bond sales in the United States, 71; 248.

Water companies, 128.
What corporation bonds are, 122 et seq.
Wholesale vs. retail bond houses, 6, 7.

THE PRINCIPLES OF BOND INVESTMENT

By LAWRENCE CHAMBERLAIN
WITH KOUNTZE BROTHERS, BANKERS, NEW YORK, N. Y.

Third edition in the press in eight months.

⁋ The extraordinary demand for Mr. Chamberlain's book may be explained in part by the following comments of the press and of individuals.

The Boston Advertiser

"This is a monumental work, and one that will remain an authority for years to come."

The New York Evening Post

"Prior to the appearance of this work, it would have been difficult to point to one such treatise that was complete in technical details, ample in historical allusion, and satisfactory in its literary features. An extended work possessing all these qualities is entitled to a very cordial reception."

The Philadelphia Public Ledger

"All classes of bonds are dealt with, and from State bonds and the history of State debt to the mathematics of bond values, the science of bond investment is presented in a scholarly yet interesting and absolutely practical manner."

Boston Transcript

"Rarely have the elements of investment been so well presented. The classification and description of securities is discriminating. The favored class, civil loans, is elaborately discussed."

Trust Companies Magazine

"A contribution to economics and a literary production that will rank the author with Walker, Adams, and Scott."

Boston Globe
"The man who makes himself familiar with the text will have a liberal financial education."

Springfield Republican
"In preparing this volume the author spent five years of such unremitting labor as steady occupation, covering every side of the business, would permit. The book was written from day to day out of the market place. The facts of the market place have been well digested, however, by the mind of a sound scholar. They are analyzed and presented in such a way as to show their significance clearly to the lay reader. . . . Mr. Chamberlain's careful and broad search has made his book the first authoritative statement of the subject."

Journal of the American Bankers' Association
"Bankers to whom the comments on the prevailing types of bonds, as bank investments, and the relation of bond prices to credit, etc., were submitted, have approved the statements made. The book forms a desirable addition to the bond department of any bank."

Investments
"The amount of concrete facts relating to securities is amazing, as the index will show, and justifies the term 'encyclopædic,' that is being applied to the book."

United States Investor
"Mr. Chamberlain's book is voluminous and has an immense amount of information on methods of bond buying and on the peculiar merits of each class of bonds."

The Boston News Bureau
"Information about bonds has in the past been divided into four classes: the raw material in the statistical manuals, a few elementary books on investments, articles in financial periodicals, and financial advertising. Obviously none of these have offered the man with funds to invest an unprejudiced opinion, to assist him in the principles of bond selection. In 'The Principles of Bond Investment' Lawrence Chamberlain has written a book clear enough to be easily understood, and substantial enough to be of practical value."

Bankers' Magazine

"Mr. Chamberlain's work deals with the general investment field, and while it is perhaps intended primarily to meet the wants of the banks and investment houses and scientific students of investments, it will, nevertheless, be found of great benefit to the individual investor. As a contribution to the permanent investment literature of the country, Mr. Chamberlain's book will be of the highest value."

A Bond Salesman

"I sold a water company bond the other day mainly on the strength of the chapter on that subject."

The Manager of a New York Bond House

"Bond houses have every reason to be grateful . . . for . . . 'The Principles of Bond Investment.' In the short time since its publication I have consulted it freely and have found just what I was looking for."

A Professor of Economics at Yale

"I have just finished reading 'The Principles of Bond Investment,' by Mr. Chamberlain, and perhaps I can best express my feelings by saying that I consider it the best book on this subject which has been written by an American."

The Dean of an Eastern University

"I shall be much surprised and disappointed if it does not very quickly become recognized as the standard treatise on bond investment."

551 pages. 19 charts. 8vo. Cloth. Price, $5 net.

Moody's Magazine Book Department

35 Nassau Street :: New York, N. Y.

**THE MOODY MAGAZINE
AND BOOK COMPANY**

35 Nassau Street :: New York

www.ingramcontent.com/pod-product-compliance
Lightning Source LLC
Chambersburg PA
CBHW020422220526
45464CB00002B/526